FAMILIES ARE FOREVER

By the same author:

A Mother's Instincts (The Aquarian Press, 1992)
The Psychic Power of Children (Rider, 1990)
Runes for Today's Woman (Foulsham, 1992)
Tarot for Today's Woman (Foulsham, 1992)

Families Are Forever

THE EXTRAORDINARY INTUITIONS
OF ORDINARY WOMEN

Cassandra Eason

Aquarian/Thorsons
An Imprint of HarperCollins*Publishers*

The Aquarian Press
An Imprint of HarperCollins*Publishers*
77–85 Fulham Palace Road,
Hammersmith, London W6 8JB

Published by The Aquarian Press 1993
1 3 5 7 9 10 8 6 4 2

A catalogue record for this book
is available from the British Library

ISBN 1 85538 259 8

Typeset by Harper Phototypesetters Limited,
Northampton, England
Printed in Great Britain by
HarperCollinsManufacturing Glasgow

To Beryl, Jack and Ivy,
part of our family forever

Contents

Introduction

Keeping in Touch

We cannot diminish the pain of losing those we love in death but we can perhaps take some consolation from the fact that love and family bonds can and do go on. This book is a collection of experiences from people who have found that families are forever. It is a book about life, not death, about hope and laughter as well as tears. Above all this book is about relationships with those we love, real relationships made up of everyday concerns and the kind of constant caring that, it seems, even death cannot erase.

We are all touched by death and there are few who would not take comfort from the knowledge that life goes on and that we may see our grandchildren grow and have families of their own, albeit from afar.

Several of the experiences recounted in this book have been collected from the archives of the Alister Hardy Research Centre for Religious and Spiritual Experience in Oxford. This and similar organizations can offer help in accepting and acknowledging experiences that go beyond the rational and material. I offer my thanks for being granted access to their records.

The majority of stories in this book, however, come from people whom I began chatting to in the street, at the supermarket, the playground or playgroup. They have a story to tell but, all too often, lack a sympathetic ear. Something very special has happened to them, but the last thing they want is to have their sanity questioned or for a professional 'ghostbuster' to dissect a treasured memory. Apart from being a writer I am just an ordinary mother of five and it seems that people feel they can talk to me. For example, on one occasion I was walking back from a playgroup in Reading (where I lived at the time) with my friend Nancy. As we pushed our buggies through the park she told me about her family 'ghosts':

'My great-granny used to read tea leaves and was very psychic, though also very prim and proper. The ability was passed down through one member of each generation.

'One of my aunts, Norah, was especially psychic. But when my own nan died, Norah suddenly lost her ability to "know" things. In fact, the ability seemed to pass to her five-year-old nephew Sam, who had shown no psychic leanings up to that point. He started to know when things were going to happen and said so, which proved a bit embarrassing at school.

'One day he told his grandad: "Nan says if you try to come and see her she won't speak to you so you can forget that idea." We all knew Grandad had taken Nan's death badly, but we didn't know that he had been contemplating suicide – which he admitted after Sam's words. We were then able to give him the extra support that we hadn't realized he needed. Nan had always been specially fond of Sam.'

Where do I interview people? In my crowded front room that doubles as my office, in people's homes, where often the experiences took place, sitting on seats in parks and playgrounds – even at the local farm park – scribbling furiously in my notebook while keeping an eye out for my children, who are usually attempting to climb into the goat pen. This is Jean's story, told me at the farm park:

'Though my mother had been ill for three months, we all thought it was gall-bladder trouble. But suddenly we were confronted with the news that she only had hours to live. After her death I was devastated with grief and with regret for the past and the things that couldn't be put right. I was especially upset when my father met someone else within a very short time. I just couldn't reconcile myself to what had happened to my mother and to life without her.

'Then six months after Mum's death I had a dream about her. I went up the steps to her house and to my amazement she was there. My sister sat by me on the settee and Dad was in his chair. I was pointing to Mum and trying to show Dad that she was there and that everything was all right and that she was fine.

'After that dream I completely stopped grieving overnight. I still see my mother in dreams and I know she is there still. Sometimes I can't remember the dreams and that is so galling. My daughter, who became very afraid of dying after her nan died so suddenly, now knows that death is not the end.'

A dream or something more? There is no way that such an experience can be verified in a laboratory – but neither can it be falsified – and surely the important part is not whether we can weigh the ectoplasm but the fact that the experience has helped a woman over her grief and a child over her fear of dying.

Psychologists might say that such an experience is all in the mind. But conversely, a psychological experience could well be triggered off by a psychic one.

This book has researched itself while I was writing other books, so if there seem to be a lot of stories from a particular geographical area it doesn't indicate an especially psychic place: it is simply that I have put roots down there for a while or even talked to a group or organization about my work and come home with a chapter or two of new experiences. You could go into any village, town or city and – if you are willing to listen sympathetically – you will hear people say: 'Yes, something like that happened to me.' It should come as no surprise, therefore, that I have gathered some of these experiences from as far away as America, Australia and India.

I found that for every traditional ghostly tale of headless cavalier or lady in white there were 50 more believable family ghosts who just dropped in to say hello. It is the very down-to-earth quality of such stories that I find so reassuring. Death seems so final, yet the love and day-to-day affection of our families offers hope that life, loving and laughter may go on.

What do these experiences teach us? One thing is that people don't seem to lose their sense of humour in the afterlife. Neither should we falsely sanctify death, for that gives it a power it should not have. I make no excuses for including stories that have made me laugh, because they capture real people and not plaster saints. I lost my own parents when I was young, so I do not make light of death or bereavement and I know the years don't take away the pain of losing those we love. But I have since seen my parents in visions and dreams – some sad, some funny. Families are made up of equal proportions of tears and laughter, so if I write with a smile on my face and a box of tissues by my side I hope I get the mix right.

Nor am I simply making a case for the believers. I am sharing with you what honest, sensible people have told me and I leave you to make up your own mind. Families don't just cease when someone dies. We are all part of our families past, present and future and even those who can't take a single word of this book seriously cannot shut themselves in a box and say 'I am what I am alone.' Our families walk with us in memories, phrases and mannerisms as well as in their achievements and oversights, just as we will walk with our descendants. Denying this link is to isolate ourselves from a whole world of love and experience.

But for many people the dead live on in more than memory. They have seen, heard, smelled and been comforted by those who have gone before who, like relatives who live abroad, must communicate only from a distance but love no less. How can a mother cease to love a baby she has borne, though that baby lived for but a second? How can a couple who shared a lifetime of joy and sorrow commune no more?

Our families, hereafter as well as here and now, keep on growing. But then love knows no limits and we can welcome the fact that our loved ones are always a part of us. Families *are* forever.

1

The Ties that Bind

Families are our greatest strength in life. Fathers, mothers, grandparents, aunts and uncles may live many miles away but they can still be counted upon to rally round in times of crisis. In times of trouble – whether we are four or 74 – it is to those to whom we are closely bound by blood that we turn.

These bonds do not end in death, they merely change. The distance between us and our loved ones may be great, but judging from the stories I have been told, love does find a way.

Much family contact from beyond flows directly to us and may continue throughout our earthly lives. Take the case of Ethel, now in her sixties. Her late grandmother has been a constant presence since she was two years old. She told me:

'My grandma came to me the night she died, although I didn't learn till later that she had died that night. It was 26th July, 1926, and I was two years and four months old. I had been sent to sleep down the road with some friends. I didn't mind because I was madly in love with their five-year-old son. I later learned that my parents had gone to Bournemouth to be with my grandmother. I woke and there was a very bright light and Granny was standing there.

' "Hello, love," she said, "I've just come to see if you are all right and tell you that tomorrow you'll be sleeping in your own bed again. Your mum and dad will be back soon. I wanted to tell you I would always look after you all your life – you must remember that because it's very important."

'After that I did talk to her often and "saw" her, though it was in a different way from when she was alive. It was like being aware of her presence. But Dad got very annoyed and tried to stop me.

I remember when I was about three some visitors had been at the house and I had been talking to my grandma and I remember he said to them, "My daughter lives on the borders of veracity" and when they were gone he was very cross. He and my mother came towards me menacingly and my father said I must stop this silliness and not talk to someone who wasn't there. "But she is here," I said. He said, "Show me."

' "There," I said and pointed, but then realized I couldn't show him. It was a different sort of seeing.

'Young as I was I knew that I was telling the truth but that no one would believe me. I had to keep silent in future. I was very upset because I didn't know how I could still talk to Granny. But she came to me and said, "Don't worry, there are lots of places we can still talk: your bedroom, the bathroom and down at the bottom of the garden behind the blackcurrant bushes."

'And so we did, and even after the bushes were cut down we found places to be together. And she has been with me all these years and is with me now as I tell you her story.'

Although sometimes a young child is involved – because children have less problems with the so-called 'barriers' of time and space – often deceased parents will come to see their grown-up child in much the same way as they did when they were alive. Frequently these parents bring words of love and consolation but, as living parents often have to do, they may come in order to give their offspring 'a good talking to' if they think it's needed.

This is what happened to Edith from Lancashire, who was very depressed after the death of her husband:

'I lost my husband when I was only 50. We'd had no children and lived more or less for each other. One particular afternoon a few weeks after his death I felt so tired I lay down on the settee and went into such a wonderful sleep I felt I didn't want to wake up. But on the chair opposite I suddenly noticed my dad smiling and looking so well. Then from behind me I felt a furious shaking and a voice saying insistently, "Come on girl, time to wake up and get on."

'Dad said, "Oh mother, leave her be. She's so tired and she's had a tough time lately." But no, mother insisted I wake up and get on with life.

'My mother has been dead 20 years and my dad 15. The strange thing was I'd been invited to Canada to visit my aunt and her children, whom I'd never seen. But I'd been hesitating. It had always been my mother's ambition to go to visit her sister in Canada, so I reasoned perhaps she wanted me to fulfil that dream for her.'

Edith added a postscript: 'I went to Canada and my relatives there gave me the friendship and love I had only previously experienced with my man.'

We cannot understand the mystery of death until we face it ourselves. In the meantime someone who has actually seen the spirit of a loved family member has a better grasp of the subject than the greatest philosopher in the land.

In fact the philosophy of this book is summed up by the matter-of-fact approach of a little girl who lost her four-year-old brother to leukaemia. In *A Mother's Instincts* I tell part of the story of Jade and her brother Calum, who died and became her phantom companion. But the story has continued.

Jade's mother, Jan, who lives on the Isle of Wight, had told me how she had seen Calum in very vivid dreams that were 'more than dreams' after his death. Jade was five when Calum died. Shortly after his death Jade started to feel his presence.

'The children always used to squabble over using the toilet,' Jan told me, 'and Jade still saw Calum there and on the stairs and she used to play with him. She'd be playing on the floor apparently alone and suddenly say "Leave that alone, Calum."

' "Every time I play games, I hear Calum in my head and when I play games he says he will play with me," Jade told her mother.

Jan very wisely encouraged her daughter to talk about Calum. People can be afraid that by accepting what a child says they are preventing him or her from accepting the reality of a sibling's death. But children can be far more realistic about death than adults, who are usually the ones who try to hide the facts. And too often it is adults' fear that prevents them from providing a child with the security to explore all aspects of bereavement. Children who talk of a lost brother or sister are offering us access to their innermost world, one we should accept with gratitude and sensitivity. And often it is children who know when it is time to let go and, even more important, that you never really lose anyone:

> When Jan mentioned a few months after Calum's death that they were thinking of trying for another baby, Jade said: 'Calum's still here, Mum. Just because you can't see him doesn't mean he's not around, you know. So the new baby will be one extra.'
>
> As with the best stories, this one goes on. Two years later I met Jan in the High Street pushing a pram. She now has a beautiful baby girl and she said that Jade has seen Calum again. One morning Jade told her: 'Calum came into my bedroom last night. He's really strong now, Mummy, stronger than when he was alive.'
>
> Jan remembers: 'Jade was sitting colouring a turtle when she told me: "Calum doesn't need me any more now." She carried on with her colouring and said: "He's really happy now."'

Many of the stories in this book prove that the parent–child bond is especially strong, even when that child is 50 and a grandmother herself.

Doris is in her seventies and her mother has been dead for more than 20 years. Yet Doris still can't escape mum's eagle eye. As we sat in her comfortable flat, Doris told me:

> 'My mum was always a very bossy woman and even when I was grown up would insist on treating me like a five year old. She had been dead for several years but I could still hear her telling me to put my vest on if it was cold though I have grandchildren of my own. One day I wanted to go to the local spiritualist church as there was a well-known medium visiting. I was in a bit of a panic

as I was behind with the dinner and so popped the greens straight into boiling water in the saucepan without washing them first. I am usually very fussy – when I was a kid Mum had drilled all the rules about "cleanliness being next to godliness," though I think for her it was the other way round and if things weren't just so you got the rough edge of her tongue.

'I thought, "Well it won't hurt for once – anyway, no one will know.'

But Doris was wrong. Later that evening the message came through loud and clear from Doris' mum via the medium. 'There's someone called Doris here and her mum has got something to say: "Fancy not washing the greens before you cooked them. Do you want to give everyone the runs?" '

Doris's story suggests that life hereafter carries on in ways not so very different from life on earth. In the next chapter I will explore that most grievous loss of all, the death of a baby or young child. Even in this most desperate case it would seem that mother love cannot be diminished though the anguish is almost too great to endure.

2

The Death of a Young Child

As a society we are, on the whole, unprepared to help parents deal with the loss of a baby either at or just after birth or when a child dies unexpectedly in childhood. The concept of children dying is so opposed to the natural order of life that even the most caring among us may cross the street rather than risk saying the wrong thing to a bereaved parent. Fortunately professionals have moved on from the days when a mother who lost a baby was told by a well-meaning nurse to go out and buy herself a new hat to make her feel better. This actually happened to a friend of mine in the early 1950s when her daughter was stillborn – though perfectly formed – at seven-and-a-half months. Strangely, Eileen, the mother, told me that she had had a feeling right from conception that the baby was a daughter and that she would lose her. I have found that this is not uncommon among mothers.

Diana, who lives in Faribault, in the US, told me:

'On October 12, 1985, I gave birth to a perfect baby boy that we named Derek Joseph. He was stillborn. I knew for quite a time before his birth that he would not live. I remember quite vividly standing over the crib of my second child Andy, who was about 15 months old at the time. I remember crying, rubbing my tummy, feeling the baby move and knowing full well that I would never see him sleeping so peacefully in his bed.

'On Sunday October 13, the day after Derek died, I had a lot of visitors. My friend Melanie, who was to have been Derek's godmother, came as soon as she was called. I asked her to go buy a white satin suit I'd seen at the store, for Derek to be buried in. While she was out I took a short nap. While I was sleeping I saw a young man with long hair dressed in a black suit. He had a face

I knew, but yet he had no face. He was walking up long, bright white steps that had only white for walls. They were not solid walls. In his arms wrapped very carefully in a white shawl was Derek. I asked him to give him back to me but he just looked over his shoulder at me.

'When he got to the top of the stairs he gave Derek to my grandmother, who died about 20 years ago. She was dressed in a blue-and-white flowered house-dress. I was on the second step from the top and my grandmother said, "You have to go back. I will take care of your son until you come to be with us."

'At that point some of my other family members came from nowhere and stood behind her. Then she turned Derek around and unwrapped the shawl so I could see him. I remember saying "But that's not what I wanted him to wear." My grandmother just smiled at Derek and he smiled at me and I knew he was safe. I will never forget how peaceful and happy he looked in the white shawl, long baptismal gown with stitching on the top and plain bonnet. He also had a ring on his finger. Grandma said again, "You have to go back."

'When Melanie returned there were more friends in the room and she gave me a packet and said the blanket was from my parents and the outfit was from herself and her husband. "The only gift we can ever give our only godchild," she said.

'When I opened the parcel, the blanket was the one Derek had on when I "saw" him with Grandma and the outfit was not the one I had sent Melanie to get. It was the one Derek had worn in my dream. When I looked shocked and dropped the box Melanie offered to drive to the store to get the one I'd wanted. But I knew this one was his.

'Later that day my husband Mark came with a plain gold band and when we went to the funeral home we placed it on Derek's finger.

'I never believed in all the "afterlife" stories about white lights and peace even though I am a Catholic and often heard my grandpa talk about the light. But I do now. I also would like to let you know that it took me a few weeks but I did write to Melanie and my mother and tell them about the dream. I have also looked at some old family photos that my mother has and when I asked her who one man was she told me he was her mother's brother who had died when he was in his early twenties. I think he was the man who carried Derek up the stairs and took his place behind Grandma. I know that this really did happen and that it will help in some way.

'I know for myself that I feel better and somewhat at ease knowing that Derek is in good hands. I believe in God but I needed my grandmother to tell me she was there to take care of him. I needed to know that he was going to get the special love that only she could give. When I think of Derek now I still sometimes become sad but now the bitterness is gone and I have a special kind of peace.

'I also believe that Derek went to heaven and that there is a reason for all things. I think that the reason Derek died was I needed to be here to help all of the others who would come after him. I have formed the Faribault Pregnancy and Infant Loss Association. It was formally founded in May 1991 and in the first seven months alone I have worked with 48 mothers from our small town as well as doing some speaking in about a 60-mile area. The funny thing is every time I even think about letting the organization fold or taking time away from it I get a call or a letter from a mom looking for information or help.'

Diana's experience helped her to come to terms with the most tragic thing that can happen to a mother: the loss of a child. Perhaps even more importantly it has allowed her to transform her pain into help for other women.

Noelene, who lives in the West Country, also found that some good came out of the tragic loss of her child, Tim.

'I gave birth to a son who was very handicapped, deaf, blind and with a hole in his heart. He died three months later.

'After his death I used to feel the weight of a baby in my arms and would cry but find no comfort for the death of my son. One day a few months later I was doing my housework when I felt the weight of a baby in my arms and I cuddled myself and him and cried. But then I felt a hand on my right shoulder, though I was in the house alone. I could see no one but I felt a calmness come over me. A few days later the same experience happened again.

Afterwards I felt greatly comforted. Then a few more days later I had the same experience for a third time. This time I spoke and I felt that Jesus was with me.

'I said, "Why, Lord?" and he answered me, "Have patience. You will have another child." Then I felt the presence of someone moving away from me and walking up the stairs in front of me. I never felt the weight of the baby in my arms again. I felt very comforted by this experience.

'Three years later to the day, I gave birth to a son. He is Downs Syndrome but he is very much a child of the Lord and I have always felt the Lord gave him to me, not to replace the son I lost but because the Lord wanted me to have a handicapped child to care for. My child brings so much joy and pleasure to all he comes in contact with.'

One way of coping with grief is through ceremony. In Mexico they celebrate *El Dia del Muerte* (the day of the dead – All Souls Day in the Catholic calendar) as Maura, who lives near Mexico City, told me:

'The day of the dead is 2nd November and for children who have died it is 1st November. People in towns, cities and villages make a path with bright yellow flowers called *Cempaxuchitl* from the cemetery to their houses to guide the dead to their homes to visit them. The houses are full of ornaments, pictures of the dead, the things that they personally used, the foods they liked, flowers and incense.

'The living pray in groups remembering the dead, asking and praying that they are in heaven living a beautiful and happy life and that their sins are forgiven. After the celebration we eat the food that was specially prepared for the dead, remembering how much they used to like these dishes.

'Everything (food, personal items, incense, flowers, pictures, etc.) is put on an altar with sweet-smelling flowers and palm leaves or other plants. We also leave water, assuming the dead will be thirsty after walking all the way from the cemetery to their family's homes.'

But when it came to a tragedy in her own life, Maura devised a special ceremony of her own which helped her and her children. She has three children, Rodrigo, 15, Omar, 10, and Pablo, who was 22 months when she wrote to me in 1992.

'When Omar was two years old I conceived without planning to do so but I was very glad. At 12 weeks I began bleeding profusely and my husband rushed me to hospital. I wanted to tell them to give me my baby afterwards, to let me see him. But I was frightened and I didn't do it. When I woke from the anaesthetic, I took courage and asked for my baby. But it was too late.

'Two years later, after many months of trying, I conceived again. I immediately told Rodrigo and Omar that they would have a little brother or sister. But things went wrong and I spent four months in bed, almost immobile. None the less I clung to the thought of my baby and couldn't even think of the possibility of my baby dying. I did everything possible to save my baby's life. I talked to him, I played music, I rubbed my stomach so he would feel me. One night at 18 weeks my waters broke and in that moment I knew my baby wouldn't live. I touched my stomach and said goodbye to him. I told him how much I loved him. My baby died inside me. That's where his short life began and where it ended.

'This time in hospital I had the courage to ask to see my baby. The gynaecologist, a friend, agreed. I saw a baby 14 cm long, perfectly formed with precious features. He looked a lot like my husband. He was a precious baby – I saw him and couldn't believe he was dead. I caressed him and held him close. He was so perfect, so beautiful, I couldn't believe it.

'When we arrived home, we had to tell Rodrigo and Omar that their baby brother had died. Rodrigo cried in silence with profound sadness. Omar sobbed without hiding his pain. The four of us went out into the yard and I told my sons to pick the star they liked the best and that the star was their little brother. Omar picked a tiny star below Orion's belt.

'One of the saddest things for me was that I never had a chance to kiss my baby while he was alive. One night, several weeks after his death I had a dream that was more than a dream. It was a live experience during my sleep. I felt my tiny baby close to me. I felt very clearly his warm body, soft and nice, his cheek touching my cheek, his skin touching mine. I held him close and kissed him, caressed him and gave him my love. He was also very loving to me. It was so real. I woke up with the sensation of his presence and still feeling his soft skin and my lips kissing him on the cheeks. I could feel his body and my hands were full of him. It was a beautiful experience, so healing. At last I could touch and kiss my baby alive and warm. The sensation I had was so full of life that I felt much better after it. My little one visited and brought me such joy and relief.'

Maura miscarried a third time but always felt these children were with her. 'When people ask me how many children I have I want to shout "five".' In September 1990 Pablo was born. The pain of Maura's miscarriages is eased by the simple ceremony of the stars, and as she says: 'When my Pablo grows he will know that his three little brothers are in the stars.'

Because the mother–child psychic bond is so strong, a mother may continue to see the child after death and at particularly stressful times over many years. Sometimes the child will continue to grow up as he or she would have done in life.

Barbara, a grandmother from Hull, has had premonitions about national and international disasters since she was a child. Yet when her first baby was due, she had no inkling of the disaster ahead. It was her father, reading the tea leaves, who felt that all would not be well. Once she had held baby Angela the bond was forged and when the baby did die Barbara believes that her love lived on. What is more, Barbara says that Angela has always been with her and, 40 years on, Barbara told me how Angela contacted her in the strangest way.

'My daughter Angela was born on 24th November, 1951, just 15 months after I married. My husband Roland was in the Army and so I was staying with my mum and dad while I was waiting for the baby to be born.

'My dad used to do tea-leaf readings and I knew Dad would never make anything up and that so many things he said came true. I do so remember it was a Thursday and I had just finished tidying up my mum's house. I felt tired. "Dad, would you like to read my cup?" I asked. I wanted to know all about the baby.

'As I gave him my cup his face looked odd and he said, "I don't feel much like reading the cups today." "Oh, Dad, you must," I insisted. Looking back I am sure he knew from that first look what would happen to my child.

'He told me I would go into the nursing home in the next few days and I was pleased as I wanted the baby to come. But he wouldn't go on. I kept on at him and so at last he said he could see a hospital ward and an operating theatre with two surgeons, the number 24 and a rather odd-looking number 8. He refused to say any more.

'My daughter was born four days later on 24th November in the nursing home, but I never related it to what Dad said. The happiness of having my first-born took over. As the days went on, the nurses moved me to an upper floor. My thoughts were still so happy. On the ninth day she weighed 8 lb 2 oz, such a beautiful baby though it was funny, I had never seen her eyes – through the whole time they were closed. Though I know all babies have blue eyes at first, I kept wanting to see them. I knew they'd be beautiful.

'Then the nurse came and said the baby had to go to hospital because she was not well. But I still didn't relate it to what Dad had said. The doctor came at 8 p.m.

' "Will she be all right?" I asked and he said her tummy was very hard but he hoped so. I could not stop crying especially when they asked me her name: we hadn't given names a thought. I had her baptized Angela in hospital, little realizing even then she was about to become an angel.

'I used to take my milk extracted with a breast pump in the ambulance to feed her. But she still never opened her eyes and I so much wanted to see them. In a way it was the hardest thing. On the Saturday I was told that two surgeons, Mr Walton and his son would operate on her – and Dad's words came flooding back. The doctors said if she could live till the Monday, she would pull through. Monday was the eighth day of the crisis (since they had discovered her illness) and Dad had seen an odd eight in the cup. "Please God," I remember praying, "let her live." But I knew now why Dad had not gone on and that there was no hope. I just wished I could see her eyes.

'Monday came and at about 3 in the afternoon my husband and I arrived at the hospital. Angela was in an oxygen tent. As we stood at the foot of the bed, Angela suddenly opened her eyes and looked straight at us as if she knew us and was saying goodbye.

'I clenched Roland's hand. "Look," I said through my tears, "they are blue and so beautiful."

'We left after a little while. All day we waited and just after 8 p.m. my sister, who was with us at Mum's that day, suddenly said she would ring the hospital to settle our minds. She came back to the room, her face full of sadness. "Sorry Babs, they were just going to ring you. Angela died at exactly 8 o'clock."

Forty years on, Barbara has never forgotten Angela though she went on to have three more children. 'I often saw Angela,' she said, 'surrounded by a beautiful blue light. I don't see her now but I know she is around me, especially if I am worried or am facing difficulties. Sometimes she will let me know she is around.'

'What do you mean?' I asked.

She told me of something that happened shortly before we met. 'I was staying in Manchester in a hotel. The video in our room wasn't working. I normally wouldn't bother to complain. It was a very nice room with a lovely picture of daffodils. Sarah, the room maid, had even left a welcoming card. When I rang through to Reception we were moved to another room. There was a beautiful picture of anemones which I had always called "Angela's flowers". I was pleased but thought no more about it. Then I picked up the room maid card. It said, "I have cleaned your room and made it as nice as I can for you. I hope you are pleased with it." It was signed Angela.'

Then Barbara told me of the first time she had sensed Angela was still around, shortly after the baby's death. Impressive though Barbara's stories were of her many premonitions, it was as we talked of Angela that I saw the real Barbara.

'On the Sunday after Angela died Roland had to go back to camp as he was in the Army all this sad time of ours. It was a lovely bright day although it was December. At 11 o'clock in the morning, I felt a bit chilly even under the big coat I had on. I remember it was a maroon one. I went upstairs to get a cardigan and as I went into the bedroom it seemed so different, happier than a few days before, with all the tears and silence. Those so very sad times I will carry with me all my days. I had a basket chair under the window. As I walked up to reach my cardigan off the chair the most beautiful blue "fairy-like" light came floating down, rested on my arm. I felt transported for a few seconds. "Oh Angela, it must be you," I thought.

'I of course reacted with a flood of tears, but felt such a comfort knowing she was with me. A good Catholic I may be but I know that life does go on in ways you can still see and sense and touch.

'I would like to give comfort to people who have lost loved ones and say talk always about them, talk to them and you will really see for yourself all the proof you need that they are always with us.'

I then asked Roland, a kind, practical North Country man if he himself had communicated with Angela. He laughed. 'Not long after Angela's death I was at home and Barbara had gone out. Suddenly all the pots and pans on the stove in the kitchen started to jump up and down. I was terrified and fled and Barbara found me sitting on the step when she came back, too scared to go in.'

Children can, as I said, have a very mature and matter-of-fact approach to death whether or not they see the dead person. Pam is now in her forties but Aileen, her mother, can recall as though it were yesterday Pam's rationalization of the situation when her older brother Geoffrey died in a road accident when he was six.

Aileen's husband's uncle died soon afterwards and Aileen was worried how Pam would react to a second death. But five-year-old Pam seemed very happy.

'Is Uncle Jack dead?' she asked.

'Yes'.

'Has he gone to heaven?'

'That's right.'

'He'll see our Geoffrey then'.

'I expect so', Aileen replied.

'Oh good,' Pamela exclaimed,' he can look after Geoffrey while God goes out with his messages.'

Aileen explains: 'Pamela knew I didn't like to leave the children alone even if I was only popping out for a moment.'

Do theologians or scientists offer better consolation than the young Pamela?

The despair a mother feels with a terminally ill child can only be imagined by those of us fortunate enough never to have experienced it. Maria lost her young son from a brain tumour when he was eight years old.

'It was a grey November day and I had driven home from the hospital where Matt was very ill. I really took a dive. I went into the deserted kitchen. The sky had turned black and there was a torrent of rain. It was so black you suddenly couldn't see the hand in front of your face. I knew I could cope with no more. "Why shouldn't I just put my head in the gas oven," I said to myself, "and end all this misery?"

'I tried to reason with myself: "But who would pull Matt through? It has to be me."

'Suddenly the room was filled with sunshine. That rotten winter day was like spring again. It was warm. A sunbeam hit me and I put my hand on the beam. I knew I would remember the moment during the days that led up to Matt's death.

'Somehow I kept going. But after Matt's death the despair hit me again. One morning, I struggled up and sat around all day exhausted and totally without purpose.

'I was swamped with disappointment for what I would never have, Matt growing up, having children, the sheer waste of all that young life and potential. Suddenly in the darkness of the late winter afternoon appeared a warm tunnel with light at the end. It got clearer and closer and there was Matt at the end. "It's so lovely to do this," said Matt. "If we never do it again at least we've done this once. I knew I'd get back to you."

'He looked so well and happy. I looked right at him and cried tears of joy. I have never had such a magic moment. I touched him and he touched me. It was lovely, really something.

'I did try to tell my husband but I knew he wouldn't believe me. He'd have thought I'd flipped.'

Linda Williamson, the medium and author of *Mediums and their Work* (Robert Hale, 1990) told me: 'Children do grow up in the world of spirit, so that a child who returns to its mother and father would have matured since its passing from the earth. They may well be brought by grandparents when they first communicate but as they become more used to making contact they are able to come on their own.

'A child who has been in spirit for some years might have grown so that the parents wouldn't recognize it. In these cases the medium will often be given a mental picture of the child as it was on earth for the purpose of recognition. A pet name would of course be just the information a child might give in order to prove its identity.'

Prue lost her two-and-a-half year old son in an accident. She didn't consult a medium but one day she met a man in a town 20 miles away who said he had a message for her, that her son was being taken care of by his uncle and that they were going on lots of 'picnic-nickies' and taking the gingerbread men.

Prue's elder brother had died some years before and 'picnic-nicky' was her son's pet word for picnics. Gingerbread men were his favourite treat.

But it is a mistake to believe that any kind of contact with a child after his or her death or any other-worldly assurances take away the grief. Support is essential to the bereaved parent. No religious belief or psychological rationalization can make up for the loss of the person or by-pass the natural healing process.

Jessica lost her young son Daniel suddenly. A fever became fatal during the night while the parents slept. It was not their fault. There was no way they could have known it was more than a mild childhood illness. But the guilt in such cases can outweigh even the grief.

'I had a vision that night in which I saw two roads and Daniel was standing at the fork. I knew which was the right way, but Daniel hesitated. Then he smiled at me and took the path that I knew would be the end of him. I couldn't stop him.'

After the funeral she said: 'I have seen Daniel. He stood in the bedroom smiling at me and he was all right. It was so lovely I knew I shouldn't grieve.'

After that Jessica seemed to get over Daniel's death very quickly, perhaps too quickly. She had another baby, a boy who was lovely but nothing like Daniel. Depression set in and eventually Jessica moved out of the family home and now only sees her surviving children once a week.

The plight of bereaved parents is accepted by almost everyone. Yet even today the grief of miscarriage is not always fully recognized. To many women the child they carry even for a few weeks or months is as real and beloved as a child who survived to full term. And mothers may continue to see children they lost in miscarriages throughout the years. Sue's lost child suddenly appeared after she had a hysterectomy. She told me: 'There was a little boy who appeared standing next to the bed. He was about six years old with black curly hair and short trousers. I started to see him after my hysterectomy. I did not want more children since I had suffered several miscarriages and the removal of my womb brought relief from severe physical problems. Nevertheless on a deeper level I mourned the loss of what I felt was the centre of my womanhood. But I didn't realize the boy who came and stood at my bedside was one of my miscarriages till a clairvoyant told me I had one son (which I do) and then said, "What about your other child who would have been six this year? I see him with you."

'When I thought back, I remembered that it was six years ago exactly since I had had a very late miscarriage, a boy. At the time I had been heartbroken. Now I realized who the little "ghost-boy" was. It is as if the hysterectomy had reawakened the psychic powers I had as a child. He still comes regularly my little curly-haired boy, but now I know who he is I am glad he is with me.'

We do not know how many women who have suffered miscarriages see their unborn child. While the physical and the emotional aspects of miscarriage may be recognized it is not

29

always easy to acknowledge the spiritual and psychic aspects whereby the foetus forms a link with the mother that can last for her lifetime.

In the case of Joshua, he thought he was seeing double when a little girl the same age as his own daughter and looking remarkably similar started appearing at dinner time and standing next to him picking bits off his plate. But three-year-old Stella was sitting opposite like an angel, though Dora, her mum, says she wasn't above pinching bits off her dad's dinner if she fancied something. Neither Dora nor Stella could see the child, but Dora wasn't entirely surprised. For Stella had been one of twins. The second twin, also a girl, was lost in a miscarriage after four months. Joshua had been with the army abroad in a trouble spot at the time and Dora, not wanting to worry him, had never told him.

Fortunately the little girl stopped coming before Joshua went for his eye test! Dora didn't explain about the other twin because she knew that, for Joshua, only earthly explanations would do.

Years later Dora went to a medium. The medium said that Dora had five children.

'No, only four,' said Dora.

'But there is a little girl standing right next to you. She is definitely one of yours. You lost her before birth.'

Of course it's a safe bet for an uncertain medium if she gets the number of your children wrong to say, 'Oh well, you must have lost – one, two, three . . .' as many women *have* suffered miscarriages. But if you have the ability and see a child or children 'standing by' a woman, be careful what you say. There is no point demonstrating your psychic powers if you are going to upset someone who would find the idea of children who were miscarried living on distressing. Psychic gifts are a double-edged sword and you need tremendous tact to know when your revelations will be of comfort and when unwelcome. Perhaps the mark of a good psychic is one who possesses sufficient intuition to gauge when to keep quiet.

Jennifer was faced with this dilemma when on her first day at as a receptionist at a private clinic in Buckinghamshire she saw the supervisor surrounded by children who looked very much like her. Some days later, Jennifer's discreet inquiries through colleagues confirmed that the supervisor had indeed suffered many late miscarriages but had now closed her mind to having children and did not wish to discuss the subject.

What can the return of infants or children who have died tell us? First and foremost that we need to support parents who have lost children for as long as they need it, which may be for the rest of their lives, not what we deem to be a 'suitable' grieving period. Nor should we not be too quick to dismiss paranormal encounters as a purely psychological process. Doctors, midwives and other health professionals are increasingly listening to mothers' intuitions, especially where there is clinical uncertainty over diagnosis.

It is important for anyone who knows a bereaved parent to be sufficiently open to allow that parent to describe any vision of or contact with the child and to accept it as *an important part of the grieving process*. Whatever our personal beliefs we should encourage and accept what parents say they have seen or sensed. We were not there; nor did we lose that child. No one can know whether what the parent saw was a manifestation or projection. But friends of bereaved parents, as well as any professionals working with them, can and should use the parents' visions and dreams of their child as a way of helping them work through the finality of the physical loss and give the lost child the same significance we would accord living family members.

3

The Death of an Older Child

The death of a teenager or young adult may occur at a time when conventional support for the family is at a minimum, especially if the death has been violent or unexpected. The loss is especially acute because the parents have been through the joys and hardships of many years of child-rearing and the turbulence of living with an adolescent, sustained by the hope of calmer years ahead, of seeing their child make a career, home and family of his or her own. The loss of possible grandchildren can be an added sorrow. Most grievously, when the lost adolescent was an only child, the family unit is wiped out overnight.

Guilt feelings can be strong in the cases of accident or suicide, which account for a high proportion of adolescent and young adult deaths.

Rufus lived in Cornwall. I include the details of his death and its aftermath because they help to explain and emphasize his post-death appearances. His mother, Christine, told me:

'I had one darling son. One Sunday afternoon he was found drowned in the sea off the promenade in Penzance in Mount's Bay. He was 16½ years old. To this day we have been unable to find out the circumstances leading to his death and this is very hard to bear. The police admitted afterwards that they didn't bother at the time. Because he was going through a "punk" phase, it didn't really matter in their eyes. This was truthfully their attitude.

'An open verdict was returned.

'The last weekend of his life Rufus had gone to stay with friends in St Ives. He didn't like us phoning to check up on him but he would always call us at least once to let us know what he was doing, his time of return and so on. He phoned on the Friday evening and again Saturday to say he was fine and would give us a bell Sunday. He did not mention that he was in Penzance. Reliable witnesses place him in the cinema from 7.30 p.m. until 9.30 p.m., but according to the police there was no sighting of him at this time.

'Usually on a Sunday if he had gone to friends, I would cook dinner as usual and save his. But that particular day I felt the most enormous sense of dread. I tried to do some sewing but my hands were shaking so much I put it away again. I didn't even make a meal.

'Looking back, I remember once when he was little looking at him sitting in an armchair watching television and laughing as the thought went through my mind "I must remember you like this." The thought frightened me but I dismissed it as irrational. The minute the last train had arrived without him we phoned every hospital and main police station between Truro and Penzance. We gave his (rather unusual) name and described his distinctive appearance. Nothing. No incidents had been reported. Yet during the afternoon and evening a large crowd (how could they?) had watched the efforts being made to bring his poor body ashore in the heavy swell and aftermath of a hurricane.

'How could they not have known at the West Cornwall Hospital in Penzance, because when we phoned his body had already been taken there? The Truro police told us curtly he was hardly a missing person. At midnight we telephoned again and they said they would send someone out for details of his description and a photograph. They assured us nothing had been reported anywhere and that undoubtedly Rufus was making his way home. The two policemen who came out again told us there was nothing to worry about and while the possibility of a road accident had occurred to me certainly the dreadful truth hadn't crossed my mind at all.

'They went away and after another hour (at 1 a.m.) we heard the police car coming back. We both went outside. One policeman was half-way down the path walking towards us. The other, holding a lighted torch, was just coming through the gate. Neither was remotely similar in build to Rufus; one was of medium height and plump, the other was slight and thin.

'Yet there were three people walking down the path, because between the two men, a head taller and looking over the shoulder of the first one, walked Rufus. I was weak with relief – after all they must have found him walking home. There he was, his big, burly, almost six-foot self. He looked at me without speaking and I noticed that he wasn't smiling. He looked half-annoyed, half-puzzled.

'I also noticed in that split second that he wasn't wearing his usual clothes. When he'd left home he was in his customary black jacket, T-shirt, jeans and boots; yet he was wearing light-coloured trousers and a lightish shirt. I found out afterwards that they were a light khaki. He was totally real and solid and as I went to rush towards him suddenly he wasn't there anymore. Then I knew.

'Later they took my husband Brian to Penzance to identify Rufus' body. On the Saturday afternoon, unknown to us, he had bought some new things in a shop in Penzance and was wearing them – a khaki shirt and trousers – when his body was recovered.

'At the time I said nothing but a few days later my husband said, "I saw Rufus that night but I didn't like to say anything in case it upset you that you hadn't seen him." I told my husband that I had seen Rufus, too. Brian saw him in exactly the same place and wearing the same clothes as I had done, but he was standing at a different angle, more side-on so he didn't see Rufus' expression as I had done. In Brian's case too Rufus simply was there and then not there.

'So we both saw him independently, totally solid and real in the same place on the path between the two policemen at the same time as they were coming to tell us. And we both saw the same clothes, clothes we did not know he possessed.

'I learned very quickly that any mention of this sighting brought at best pity and at worst downright hostility. I tried to talk to the local vicar, but he merely said it was wishful thinking. Others said our minds were under stress. We were very close and loved Rufus more than anything in the world. I believe Rufus knew not only the tragedy of his death but that the unresolved circumstances would always torment us, what with all the people who had been negligent about his whereabouts and the wicked treatment we received from the police.

'I believe it was Rufus' way of saying "I'm OK" because he

knew how terrified I would be that he had ceased to exist and gone into oblivion.

'One other thing was strange: some time later I was put in touch with the Compassionate Friends and through them a group called Parents of Murdered Children. We write to each other and help each other as best we can. Although the way Rufus died was never established, the group felt they could offer support. One lady I write to, Sheila, answered one of my early letters by return of post. In my letter I had told her how I missed Rufus coming home from work, how he would always say, "Hello my flower" which was his special greeting for me. As far as I know the expression is used more in the West Country than elsewhere.

'Early in the morning before my letter had arrived Sheila had seen the rest of the family off to work and decided to get a bit more sleep. She always slept badly during the night, so she dozed off in the chair and dreamed that her (dead) son Darren had come back into the house with a friend. The boys were larking around, talking and laughing and she called out to Darren to introduce his new friend. She said he came in with this boy and said, "This is Rufus, Mum." Rufus gave her a brilliant smile and said, "Hello, my old flower."

'Sheila had laughed and told him "Not so much of the old!" and he replied, "But that's what I call my mum."

'A few hours later she received my letter telling her about him. Also in the dream Rufus had a boot-lace missing, which he did, and she searched for a new one for him. She hadn't heard the expression "old flower" before.

'I suppose it might have been telepathy, grief making us closer. but she has dreamed of them several times, always together. In one they told her they were looking after Darren's grandfather who had just died.'

How could Rufus' parents have seen him wearing clothes he had only bought the weekend he died? Both father and mother saw him independently walking between the policemen. Rufus always let his parents know he was safe in life, why not in death?

A few months later I heard from Christine again.

'Rufus was very close to my mother, his grandmother, and went to see her as often as he could. She lives with her sister in a cottage in a village several miles from our home.

'During the morning she was sitting in her chair and as she turned her head she saw Rufus standing at her side. She said he was bending down – he was quite tall – with his hands on his knees, just looking at her with a serious expression on his face. He was bare-chested as if he had been gardening or something like that and was wearing jeans and trainers. She told me, "I put out my hand to him and said 'Oh Rufus' and then he was gone." She was most indignant when I asked her if she was sure about this, but I had to be sure. Mother swears she was wide awake at the time.

'It is almost exactly three-and-a-half years since the night we saw him and he came in the gate with the two policemen. He came to us when he knew we were about to hear terrible news and, writing this now, something has occurred to me.

'I have seen him twice in dreams but only actually seen him the once and I realize how important and precious that is, as does my husband. Last October we had to take the sad decision to have his darling old dog Cassie put to sleep. Rufus chose the name after Prince Caspian in the Narnia books. Before Rufus went out he used to hug Cassie and say, "Take care of him until I get back" and we did because we loved the dog, too. Two days afterwards I dreamed that Rufus was standing on the top of the stairs. He looked very serious and as I went up the stairs towards him he put his hand up gently as if to stop me getting closer and said, "You know I won't be staying, Mum," and I believe he had come back for his beloved dog.'

Dream, vision, what-have-you – this was a reminder for Rufus' mother of what a kind, loving boy he was.

'Could I have prevented it?' is the unspoken reproach on many parents' lips in the case of the sudden or violent death of their offspring. Often parents may have a premonition of disaster but have been unable to stop their teenager from living his or her own life. All of us who have teenagers have waited for the key in the lock and imagined a thousand horrors waiting to ensnare the absent adolescent. Yet we have to let our children grow and go from us. All we can hope is that we have instilled in them somewhere some of the beliefs we hold dear to protect them.

Yet, ironically, these premonitions may prepare parents and make some sense of a tragedy. Hannah, who lives in Hampshire, told me:

'At the beginning of November I had a dream about the death of our son although it seemed very vague the next morning. A few days later I had another dream. I woke to remember it much more clearly than the first. It was again regarding the death of our son. This time I was surrounded by people, all very upset. The strange thing was I was comforting them and reassuring them that everything was all right. Death, I explained, was nothing to worry about and Mark would be fine. When experiencing a dream of this kind one usually wakes with feelings of concern, considering it more of a nightmare. But this was not so. I felt no apprehension at all.

'On 10th November, 1984, the dream became a reality. We lost our only son Mark in a road accident shortly before his eighteenth birthday. He and I enjoyed a close, loving relationship and I did find myself reassuring others that all would be well. My calmness amazed those around me but not myself.

'During the following months many things happened that seemed to be pointing to the fact that Mark was still with us. One wonders, of course, if it isn't just wishful thinking. But everything that has happened has made us rethink our ideas of life and death.

'The most remarkable incident for me concerns a horse called Sam who had stayed with us for a year during which time Mark had grown very fond of her. He rode her, brought her in at night and even nicknamed her Fluff. It was rather a ridiculous name for a 16-2 hands thoroughbred but it stemmed from the fact she grew a very fluffy coat in winter. After Mark's death she returned to her original home where she was looked after by a friend of mine.

'One morning my friend was exercising one of the horses on land that had been cleared of trees (and so had good visibility). The other horses including Sam were back at the farm grazing in the field. On my friend's return she met the young lady who worked at the farmhouse and who had been out walking the dogs. The young lady asked my friend whom she had been riding with as she had seen her with a young man on a horse that looked like Sam. But on her return the girl realized this could not have been, as Sam was still in the field. My friend was puzzled, as at no time during the ride had she seen anyone except the young lady walking the dogs. She thought at once it had been Mark with her.

'No one can ever prove any of this, but the interesting thing was that the young lady never knew us or about our son or the horse having been with us. What she saw had nothing to do with any prior knowledge or preconceived ideas.

'Call it sixth sense, call it what you like, but I have no doubt that it was Mark. When my friend told me I was unsure whether to voice my feelings but then I realized she had experienced the same feelings. Since then she has experienced similar things on other occasions, but only when she is with the horses.'

Shortly after Mark's death Hannah found herself writing a book of poems dedicated to his memory. She says: 'I do not have any gift for writing. All I did was write them down. From where the poems came I do not know but I felt that Mark was impressing me with the words. What I do know is that until that time I had not been capable of such things. It was just like a tape-recorder in my head. In fact I could have done with a rewind or slow-down button at times.'

Hannah has sent copies of her poetry to other bereaved parents who have asked her for help. She believes it is one of the good things to come from Mark's death.

In Hannah's case the premonition spoke of disaster only days away though no time was given. But what if the premonition speaks of loss that does not come about for many years? What then can a mother do when every mishap raises the question 'Is this the time?' Connie lives in a warm, comfortable little house on the Isle of Wight. It is 25 years since her son Peter died but in her case she had waited for disaster to strike over a period of many years.

She told me:

'All upsets and hurts pass in time. I was demented when Peter died at 23. Yet I had always known I could not keep him. From the minute Peter was put in my arms after he was born, I knew he would die, and there were many close shaves in his young life when I thought the time had come.

'When he was quite young he nearly drowned in the boating lake at Ryde. He was going under for the third time when someone managed to pull him out.

'When Peter was eight, a family in the next street had a cat with a litter of new kittens, so he went with their little boy to see them. The house was only in the next street, but I didn't know the boy's mum had slipped out to the shops and left the boys alone.

'About half an hour later I was standing in the kitchen when I heard the wail of a fire engine. "Peter," I called out. "Don't be daft," my husband told me, "the fire engine could be going anywhere."

'But I knew, and I ran to the next street. Sure enough the boys were outside. A soldier had gone in to rescue them. The other boy had been playing with matches and accidentally set the place on fire. The house was gutted but no one was harmed.

'Every time Peter went out of the door I feared I would never see him again. But what could I do? It wasn't fair to smother him. I knew I had to encourage him to live his life however short it might be. Peter was always very special, a golden child. We never had a cross word and if I gave him advice he listened to it. He was a wonderful child. Even when he was only three or four years old he would be pedalling up to the almshouses on his little trike to talk to the old ladies or go to the corner shop for them. But he would never take any money as a reward. "Keep your pennies," he told them, "I've got a daddy."

'As he got older he would be first down the road to clear the snow from the almshouse doors. Even as a teenager when he started work, the money for his keep was always in my hand and he never gave me cause for grief.

'Peter married when he was 21. His son was only two months old when Peter was killed. He desperately wanted a son of his own to carry on after him. It was as if he knew he was running out of time. Not long after the baby was born he told his wife, "I won't die in my bed. I'll die in a road accident." It was as if he was trying to prepare her.

'Peter started to use his bike to travel to work because he wanted to save money for Christmas presents for the baby. The day before he died he took his bike into the shop and had it checked, lights, brakes, everything.

'He popped in on his way home and I said, "Don't use the bike tomorrow. Please use the bus, just tomorrow," and he said he would. But he didn't. A car ran into the back of him the next day and he was killed.

'In a strange way it was a relief when he died. I had been fearing the moment so long. It was strange because a couple of months before he died I'd relaxed.

'Even so I was devastated. I went nearly mad when he died. But not long after the accident a woman who said she was a medium came to see me because she said she had something to tell me. A young man had suddenly appeared to her that day and wanted to let me know he was all right. He was wearing an awful lavender-coloured suit with big drapes, she said. He was showing her the lapels of the suit and smiling.

'Then I knew Peter wasn't gone from me. He had to have his clothes made specially because he was so tall. This particular suit I absolutely loathed. He made quite a joke of my dislike because it was so rare for us to disagree about anything. He would parade himself in front of me in it, showing me those awful lavender drapes.

'It made me laugh when she told me. It was the one thing that convinced me Peter was still around because she hadn't even known Peter and couldn't possibly have known our private joke.

'After Peter died, I used to dream of him. Once he was in an attic; a filthy old room. There was a swivel mirror and suddenly I heard Peter's voice perfectly clear: "Mum".

'I turned and in the mirror I saw his face. It was a dream but not a dream as such. It was so real. I have a mirror just the same in my bedroom and I often wonder if I shall see his face in it some day. But I suppose I don't need to any more.

'He is here with me still but only as he always was in life, popping in to say "hello" and going on his way. You don't lose the love of a child even in spirit by letting him go forward. I was proud to be his mother. I rarely go to the cemetery because he is not there. A child is special and for you to nurture and let him go when the time comes, however short.

'People say to me, "Is it worse to lose a child or a husband?" for my husband died three years later. He never got over Peter's death. I say it's worst when the first one goes, for it breaks up the family. Even if the separate family members aren't close there is the family link. Once it's broken by death it's so hard for those left to carry on. Part of you dies if you let it, so you mustn't. But that first year is the worst.'

Parents of children who die violently may go from medium to medium seeking some explanation or even an assurance that the death wasn't suicide, but the unfinished business remains. For some parents a reliable medium may be of immense help and comfort, but many of us can make the link ourselves if we trust our intuitions. It is perhaps the personal signs, whether full-blown visitations or even just hints that the adult child is around and happy, that can with time help heal the wounds.

Even when a child is an adult the pain of losing him or her can be unbearable. One couple lost their 35-year-old son John when the plane he was flying solo crashed. No explanation could be found in terms of mechanical failure of the plane. The unspoken question was had John committed suicide and, if so, why? Mediums couldn't explain the crash but evidence came of John's care for his family in an unexpected way.

John's diver's watch had survived the crash, although the strap was severed. Phil, his father, put the watch away in a chest of drawer's in John's old room, unable to look at it. A few days later, however, Phil's own watch came undone and fell into the sea and he found himself led to the drawer. There next to his son's watch was a brand-new strap that neither Phil nor his wife had seen before. Now when Phil wears it he feels close to his son and is sure that the appearance of the new strap was John's way of reassuring his parents. In his efforts to contact John through a medium Phil had overlooked his own link with his deceased child.

Of course it's very easy to dismiss mediums as frauds. Yet supposing they come up with information even the person they are reading for doesn't know? A story told to me by the widow of George Finn, a medium from Dorset, is a good example of this. He was trying to help a couple whose son had died and told them he could see a pair of brown shoes by a distinctive carved wooden chair. They didn't understand and went away disappointed. But a week later the father phoned George. He had been to the workshop where his son was employed and for the first time saw his son's flat which was over the workshop. The pair of brown shoes were standing next to the exact chair George had described.

Spooky? No – one of those hints that show a beloved son is saying 'I'm OK, Mum and Dad. I made it.'

The real point of such encounters, whether direct or 'transmitted' via a third party, is to affirm that our loved one is still there though unseen and that love is more powerful than death.

What can we do to help in cases of the death of a teenager or young adult? Because of the tremendous guilt (albeit unwarranted) that may be involved when a teenager or young adult dies as well as the reminder of unfulfilled potential, the parent may need to go over the tragedy many, many times. So any help that is offered, whether by a reliable medium, health professional or friend must be continuing or it can stir up feelings that, unworked through, may be very destructive.

Of course all teenagers do not die violently or suddenly. Doreen was 18 when she died of leukaemia after a long struggle against her illness. Knowing an illness is terminal does not make the final loss any easier to bear. If the teenager has grown progressively sicker there is not even a final memory of the beloved child well and strong. So the experience of Doreen's grandmother was doubly precious in that she saw her beloved granddaughter full of joy once more.

'In the early evening I had the amazing experience of "seeing" my granddaughter, who had died the previous evening.

'Supported by an unseen force in a half-reclining position, Doreen was looking upwards in a joy and wonder such as I have never seen before. At the same time I heard in my mind the words "Doreen is happy" and I felt my courage come flooding back.

'It was all over in a few seconds but was the most precious moment of my life.'

We cannot say for certain where psychology ends and the spiritual begins. The fact that such encounters are enriching, uplifting and healing is surely what matters.

4

Ghostly Grandparents

It's not just children who see their grandparents after death. And it's not surprising that a relationship that is usually so warm and positive in life should endure beyond it. Grandparents are the most frequently seen returning family members. Some act as guardian angels (I've included these in a later chapter when I look at reasons *why* family members appear). Here the grandparents are in death much as they were in life: loving, nagging, cajoling and prompting.

Jane is an experienced social worker in her mid-thirties living in the south of England. She had always been very close to her grandmother and so the old woman's sudden death came as a great shock. A day or two after the funeral, Jane was standing in her kitchen making shepherd's pies for her grandad to put in his freezer.

'Grandad wasn't a great cook and I knew Gran would have wanted me to make sure he got a hot meal every day. But all the time I was cooking I could feel my gran hovering behind me, just as she always used to. If I were doing something wrong she would never come right out and say anything but stand there fidgeting until at last I would stop and say, "OK Gran, what is it then?" and she would take over.

'At last I said, "Look Gran, I just can't cope. Please leave me alone." And I couldn't cope, not right then, not with Gran's death and the funeral and sensing her there as she always was, though I knew she'd never do anything to hurt me.

'I felt her presence leave.

'I woke in the night from a troubled sleep and it was as if I could hear her right there talking to me. "You know your grandad won't eat shepherd's pie without gravy."

'Of course that was it. That was what she had been trying to tell me. I sank back, feeling more at peace, and slept properly for the first time since Gran had died. I got up early and made gravy, which I put on top of each pie, smiling to myself for Gran was very near. Grandad enjoyed the pies, though of course they weren't as good as Gran's.'

Perhaps the ghostly grandparent is the most easily accepted and also the most rewarding contact from beyond. For a grandparent/grandchild relationship is often free of the conflicts that crop up between parents and children.

Sometimes the encounter between grandparent and grandchild is a simple one-off appearance and not even at a time of particular stress or sorrow. Teresa, who works for an international publishing house, was visited when she was a child.

'We lived in the country when I was young. When I was nine I was walking along the lane with a friend. An old lady came towards us and said, "Hello girls."

'It was pretty unusual to meet anyone out walking where we lived and she seemed very familiar. I experienced a lovely warm feeling as she passed us.

'It was only as she passed us I realized it was my great-grandmother who had died when I was three. I recognized her from the photos we had round our house. But when I turned round she was gone. It was only afterwards I felt frightened. Great-grandma was a person who always took a lively interest in the family so I suppose she was just keeping an eye on me – a sobering thought!'

Rita, who lives in Oklahoma in the US, is a writer, researcher, mother of ten (seven of whom are adopted) and editor of the newsletter for AASK (American Association for Kids with Special Needs). She describes how her beloved grandfather appeared not to one but five different relatives after his death – surely a record for taking your duties seriously. But then, as Rita explains, he was a pretty special grandfather who firmly but lovingly sat at the head of a close-knit family. So why should death change the natural order?

'The first other-worldly contact with "Grandee", as we always called him, came the morning he died,' Rita recalls. 'It was a beautiful mild Saturday morning in Downey (a Los Angeles suburb) on May 22, 1971. I was 14 years old and sleeping late. I was awakened by the sound of my youngest sister's voice. Jo-Jo, aged five, was talking in her sleep. Over and over again she was saying, "What Grandee? What did you say? Speak up, I can't hear you."

'I told Jo-Jo to be quiet – it was only a dream.

'But Jo-Jo, wide awake now, was convinced she had been speaking to her grandfather.

'A little while later the phone rang. I sat up instantly and for some reason yelled, "It's Grandmother."

'I didn't know how I knew that but I did. Before even picking up the phone I knew something was wrong with my beloved Grandee. There was no logical reason for me to think that way. Living half-way across the country in Oklahoma, he had been in perfect health the last time I'd seen him.

'I said, "Hello Grandmother," without waiting to see if it really was her. If she was surprised she didn't let on. Her voice sounded calm – too calm. "Give the phone to your father," she said. Within seconds his face told us the news. Grandee had died just a short time before from a massive and sudden heart attack. Grandmother told Dad that she had been making Grandee's breakfast while he showered. When he came into the kitchen he stumbled and then fell to the ground clutching his chest. As he breathed his last, he mumbled something that Grandmother could not hear. She put her ear close to his mouth and asked him to repeat it but it was too late. He was dead. Her description of the mumbling and the time it happened corresponded exactly to Jo-Jo's dream in every detail, especially the fact that he was mumbling something she couldn't understand.'

A year later, Rita believes, her grandfather came to help her to come to terms with his death.

'Though everyone kept telling me Grandee was dead, deep

down I didn't believe it. One evening about a year after he died I was babysitting a few miles from home at a house I had never visited before. By 9 p.m. both girls were asleep and I had three hours to pass before the parents came home. The two-bedroom stucco house was quiet and still so I turned off all the lights except for a lamp by the phone, stretched out on the sofa and phoned my boyfriend.

'I first noticed the rocking chair as I was dialling. It was funny I hadn't noticed it before as it was an exact replica of a rocking chair my grandfather had owned. Even the old blue cushion tied to the seat of this one was like Grandee's.

'As I started to talk to my boyfriend, the rocker began to move. My innate capacity to ignore painful reality allowed me to ignore it at first. But the rocker continued to rock, slowly and steadily, all by itself.

'It was the way it was moving that finally caught my attention. It was Grandee's unique rocking motion. I told my boyfriend what was happening not six feet away from me. I knew he wouldn't doubt my sanity and I made him promise to phone the police if the phone connection was broken.

'My boyfriend suggested possible explanations – one of the girls playing a trick; a breeze; an earthquake – all were checked and discounted. That left only one thing to do. The chair had to be touched. I had to check for strings, wires and even batteries. I was determined to get to the bottom of the mystery.

'Several attempts failed. There was nothing tangible preventing me, just a strong feeling that the chair should not be touched. The closer I moved to the chair the stronger the conviction became.

'I put the phone receiver in my lap and closed my eyes. I cleared my mind and waited, no longer the least bit afraid. Gradually a single thought came: "Grandee is dead. He is gone." And I knew the time had come to let go of my very best friend.

'I opened my eyes to see the chair once more. Feeling my grandfather's presence all around me I said goodbye through my tears. Almost immediately the chair was still. Today I own Grandee's oak rocking chair.

'Grandee also appeared to my favourite uncle, one of his sons, in a dream. It was the most realistic dream my uncle had ever had and in it my grandfather told him to stop grieving and accept his death.

'There is yet a fourth person my grandfather contacted after his death, my cousin Will. Will believes that since Grandee died he has guided and protected him from all danger and harm. One of Will's most prized possessions was a 1957 Pontiac car that his grandfather had bequeathed him.

'Will admits that he has a "lead foot" and drives the car very fast, too fast, in spite of earthly counsel to the contrary. One night Will was passing through Eufaula, Grandee's old home town, and was about to turn off the highway. Before he got to the turn, the voice that had been with Will since Grandee died told him to slow down at once, which Will did.

'A fork of lightning hit the sign at the corner and Will says if he hadn't listened to Grandee and slowed down at that precise moment the lightning would have gone right through the car.

'The fifth and final contact that I know of was with me in 1984. I was terribly discouraged after having tried to adopt a special needs child for four years. I was ready to quit.

'Grandee never gave up on anything he wanted, "Where there's a will there's a way" was part of his legacy to us. I have drawn strength from Grandee whenever I feel like giving up.

'My grandfather came to me in a dream and told me I was not allowed to give up on a child who needed us. After all, the child could not come to me. Though the dream was not terribly precise I was positive I was in direct communication with my Grandee. He asked why I would consider giving up? Who taught me such a thing? Not from him, certainly.

'I woke up feeling embarrassed that I had ever allowed myself to become discouraged. I was supremely confident from then on. Seven months later, baby Antonio came to us. He has big brown eyes that reflect his Cherokee heritage. We thank Antonio's great-grandfather, our Grandee, without whose legacy and wise words we might never have persevered and found our little miracle.

'All of us with whom Grandee made contact were non-believers in this sort of "from beyond-the-grave" thing. Nor has any of my family members, including myself, ever had any other contacts with anyone else.'

Small children seem to have special access to their grandparents and find death no barrier to the everyday contact they take for granted. Tracey, who lives in Buckinghamshire, told me:

'My daughter Tanya wasn't more than three when my Dad died from a heart attack. Tanya has always been very articulate for her age. Indeed, I have better conversations with her than with many adults!

'We were living about six miles from my parents when my father died unexpectedly. On the evening before he died Tanya kept insisting that she should talk on the phone to her grandad, to whom she was very close. But I said we'd pop round to see Nanny and Grandad in the morning as we didn't have a telephone where we were living. But Tanya wouldn't give in and so at last we went down to the phone-box to ring them. Dad was in the middle of decorating the kitchen and Mum was helping him. They were laughing because the tiles kept falling off the wall.

'After Tanya had spoken to her grandparents I bathed her and put her to bed, though unusually she kept screaming that she didn't want to sleep. She was very restless even after she had dropped off. At exactly 10.50 p.m. – I don't know why I looked at the clock – Tanya woke up screaming and crying. I asked her what was wrong but I couldn't make any sense of what she was saying through her tears. She eventually fell into a troubled sleep in my arms. I tiptoed out of the room but I couldn't settle.

'Not long after, my cousin knocked at the door. "It's your dad," he told me. "He's had a heart attack."

'I was just so thankful Tanya had persuaded me to ring my mum and dad that evening. The hardest thing was accepting that Dad would never come walking through the door again. I discovered that Dad had died at precisely 10.50.

'After my father's death Tanya often used to sit on her bed and hold conversations with him or talk to his photo on the sideboard. I put this down to imagination. But then my mum offered to look after Tanya while I was at work. When I collected Tanya in the evening Mum told me that during the afternoon Tanya had gone into a "daze". She seemed to look straight through Mum to someone beyond her and was nodding her head and answering

"Yes" and "That's right." Mum asked Tanya what was wrong but the only answer she got was "Shh, Nanny."

'After about 10 minutes of this Tanya blinked and shouted, "I wish you wouldn't talk to me when I'm talking to Grandad."

'Mum was quite taken aback.

'Quite recently Mum told me that on another occasion when Tanya was staying with her she started to shout, "Open the back door and let him in please." "Let who in?" Mum asked. "I can't hear anyone there."

' "Yes, there is. Grandad's outside and he says hurry up, he wants to come in."

'Mum says she froze, so Tanya tutted and opened the door herself. "Oh it's all right. He says he'll come back another day." And then Tanya apparently carried on playing.

'Quite recently I was driving my Dad's old car. As we were going along Tanya suddenly unstrapped herself, leaned forward between the driver's and passenger's seat and cuddled the passenger seat.

'I asked her what she was doing, as she is always very sensible about staying in her seat belt, and she replied, "Grandad was sitting next to you, Mum, so I was giving him a cuddle. But he's gone now." And she climbed back into her seat for the rest of the journey.

'About a week before Christmas Tanya was sitting in bed and I was tucking her up when she suddenly said, "Oh, hello, Grandad." Then she just smiled and fell asleep.

'When Tanya got up next morning she came running in and said: "Grandad came to see me last night."

'I said: "I know. What did he say?"

' "He told me to be a good girl for Father Christmas and he gave me pennies. And a lady, Grandad's mummy, gave me a ticket and put it on top of the pennies."

'I couldn't understand what Tanya meant, so I asked Mum.

'Mum found an old photo of her wedding day and there was Dad's mum, as well as her own, standing next to them. I asked if Tanya had seen the picture but Mum said that she hadn't because it had been upstairs in the attic for years.

'I borrowed the photo and showed it to Tanya. She pointed out my dad, though he was of course much younger then, but was really only interested in the woman next to him. "Look,

Mummy, that's the lady I told you who gave me the ticket. She's Grandad's mummy, you know." My gran had died before I was born.

This enduring and positive presence of deceased grandparents in the lives of grandchildren, young and adult, can be a source of comfort in a changing world. Simply holding some little treasure or going to a favourite shared place may be enough to trigger off the connection. But don't *expect* to see your gran or grandad – indeed it's not a good idea to try to conjure up anything other than a positive feeling of warmth and love. For every story I receive of an actual visitation I get 20 where the contact is more fleeting but no less real: a scent, a glimpse, a 'feeling' that gran is there and approves.

Above all, don't forget that sometimes a grandparent can be scathing and may want to remind the younger generation of what it has to be thankful for. Pat was very proud when her son Robert got a place in the Junior County cricket team and she fondly imagined Grandad, an enthusiastic cricketer, looking down from his cloud with pride.

But the message she received through a medium was brief and sharp: 'All these new-fangled things they wear to protect themselves,' grumbled the old man, obviously offended by the headguards and other devices. 'Load of softies. In my day we stood and took the ball like a man.'

5

Till Death Us Do Part?

The partnership between two people – one that may last three quarters of a lifetime – is bound to be forged with unbreakable bonds. In this chapter I look at the ups and downs of married life and see the tears, love and laughter that survive.

Can you fix this plug?/lend me the milk money?/hold my hand at the dentist? are the conversational gems that make up 95 per cent of the fabric of married life. And these conversations, reassuringly ordinary, comfortingly banal, can continue in the afterlife – as Paula discovered.

Paula, in her early fifties, went along to a spiritualist church in Berkshire and found that her hubby had more than a few things to say on the DIY front. The place was apparently falling down without him, according to the messages relayed by the medium.

'There is trouble with a door that is sticking,' the medium relayed.

'Yes,' Paula had to admit. A friend had painted a door for her that weekend but it hadn't been left to dry properly and now it was sticking.

Her husband, the handyman, was leaving Paula in no doubt that this message came from him:

'Your husband says he used to blow down something with a spout and make a tune,' the medium said, and his puzzled frown proclaimed that he could make head nor tail of the message.

But Paula smiled. 'Oh yes, Harry used to make music by blowing down the teapot spout. It was his party piece.'

Here we leave the realms of discussion about mediums' mind-reading. Why on earth should Paula be thinking of such an obscure fact? But Harry hadn't finished.

'Your husband says that there is something wrong with the wall in the living room that is getting on his nerves.'

'That's right,' said Paula. 'There's a piece of wallpaper hanging off. I have been meaning to get it fixed.'

It is these naggings and scoldings that make us smile and see that death cannot snuff out the bantering humour that is the cement of married life.

Doris, whom we met in Chapter 1, told me a story about her late husband. She recalled that one afternoon she'd gone shopping for a new pair of shoes but came home with a couple of cheap pairs instead, congratulating herself on saving a few pounds though she didn't need to. But within a few minutes she realized her mistake. The shoes crippled her and, pushing them in the cupboard, she put on her old pair to go along to her local spiritualist meeting. There was a new medium that evening, and he instantly homed in on her.

'I've got your late husband here. He says: "Fancy wasting your money on those cheap shoes. You know cheap shoes cripple you so you wasted your money after all." '

Doris laughed as she told me: 'It was Trev's very expression and tone of voice. I knew it was him.'

Again, evidence from a third party can answer many cynics who say such contact is 'all in the mind'. Equally, though more rarely, direct contact between husband and wife can be witnessed by an outsider.

Not long after the death of her husband, Elsie, who lives in Avon, went on holiday to a hotel on the south coast of England with her friend May. They shared a room. 'One morning I woke up very early and, because May was asleep in the other bed, I was unable to put the light on to read. I sat against the pillows regretting I hadn't come on holiday alone.

'Suddenly the bedroom door opened and in walked my husband. I was totally shocked. I said: "I thought you were dead. I shouldn't be here if you are alive."

'I had no idea how I should explain to my husband's firm, who were paying for the holiday. But my husband told me not to worry and he came and sat behind me. I lay back in his arms on the pillow and we talked of many things.

'Suddenly May looked up and said, "Oh don't mind me, I'll face the wall and I won't listen," and that is what she did. We continued talking long after daylight and then I went to sleep, totally comforted.

'May and I didn't discuss the incident until some two years later. She had never told anyone but we both knew it had really happened.'

It was the practical issues that preoccupied Dorothy, who lives in Bristol, during the period that led up to her husband's death.

'The feelings that I experienced for about 18 months before my husband died I had felt several times before. It was then always something to do with one of the children. On those occasions this feeling lasted one or two days at the most, but once whatever it was that was wrong made itself known these feelings would disappear. I say it is a feeling but it is like a weight which seems to envelop me and lays heavy on me. This feeling was with me on and off for those months prior to my husband's death.

'I would wake in the night and think, "I won't like being in the house by myself."

'On the actual day that my husband died, twice I nearly replied sharply to something he said but both times a voice clearly said to me, "Don't cause an argument." '

But her husband's fatal road accident was not the end. 'I was awakened not long after my husband's death by a kiss which was so light that it felt like brushing a baby's cheek. Then the covers seemed to move and my husband got into bed with me. I became frightened and then seemed to fall back on the bed with a bump, which awakened me. I was so angry with myself for being frightened and spoiling the moment. There are times still when I sense my husband around and he has helped me many times I know.

'We had been married for 34 years and knew each other for 48. Since my husband was only 56 when he died I had known him for most of his life.'

It is not surprising that a link that has lasted half a lifetime or more should not cease with the death of the earthly body.

Sally's story is especially interesting because it demonstrates the telepathic link that can sometimes exist between husband and wife in life. We can speculate that such psychic links make it easier to accept post-death contact. Sally is in her sixties and a busy grandmother, so not at all in the category that might be regarded as 'alone with her memories'. But she is very wary whom she tells about her husband Bill's constant presence, because she has discovered that she is too often labelled a cranky widow if she admits to having him still in her life.

'My husband Bill was in hospital for an emergency operation. He lost so much blood he nearly died. I could not be with him; I had to go to work because we had no money. But suddenly I had a dreadful feeling and I found myself walking round and round the flat saying "You've got to get well and come home, Bill," over and over again.

'The moment I got to work I phoned the hospital. The nurse told me Bill had lost consciousness and when he was revived had told her he had gone to the "pearly gates". Bill later told me they really were pearly. All the pain was gone and it was so beautiful but he could hear a voice saying "You've got to get well and come home, Bill," over and over again. So he fought to come back and the pain was strong again.

'He never fully recovered and was ill on and off for years. As Bill lay dying he couldn't talk much but he wrote little notes to me. "Always remember I love you." "I'm not afraid to die because I've seen the pearly gates."

'Years later I went with a friend of my younger daughter to a spiritualist meeting. The medium pointed to me and said, "You've got your late husband's wallet in your bag. He says it needs stitching."

'The stitching had come undone a couple of weeks before and I'd been meaning to get it repaired. So I laughed. But the medium wasn't finished.

"Your husband says that nightdress you don't like needs mending too."

'That afternoon I'd been in my bedroom sorting jumble. There was a mauve nightdress I hadn't worn since Bill died. I'd been given it by a relative but I'd always felt that mauve was an unlucky colour for me, though Bill used to laugh at me for being superstitious. It was brushed nylon and the seam had come undone but I'd thought as I pushed it in the jumble bag that whoever bought it could mend it.

'Bill sent a third message that evening: that I'd got some premium bonds I was going to cash in, but I mustn't on any account. I'd had them for ages and hadn't won a thing so I'd been thinking only that week that I might as well have the cash instead.

'The bonds did come up, not big amounts but it was very useful, so I was glad I'd taken Bill's advice.'

At first, when grief is acute, it is not always possible to recognize a partner's attempts to offer reassurance and evidence of continuing love. Ruth's husband was first seen after his death by their four-year-old surrogate niece.

Ruth is now in her nineties and lives in Dorset. She married her first husband Frederick in 1940, though originally she declined his proposal because she thought he was 'too tidy'. Once he'd explained that it was his aunt who insisted on tidying up after him the nuptials went ahead. He and Ruth shared 28 happy years of marriage. She can recall even now how hard it was when her beloved husband died from pneumonia.

'Though I have no children of my own I have always been closely involved with other people's. When Frederick died, the family across the road proved an inestimable comfort and help to me, especially the children. Esther, who was just turned four, was over with me one day watching television. Suddenly but quite quietly she said, "You know Uncle Fred isn't dead. He's just above your head but the light is so bright you can't see him." And she went on looking at TV as though it was the most natural thing in the world. I did not question her but that line came to me, "'Tis only the splendour of light hideth Thee" and I felt at peace.'

A year later Ruth herself sensed her husband's presence early in the morning. 'Usually in the morning I wake quickly and am at once alert. One morning, however, I wakened slowly as though coming from a distance. At the same time I was conscious of a feeling of intense happiness. Something beyond happiness, indescribable. I also was aware of a scent, quite strong at first but which gradually faded as I became fully awake. The happiness remained. I lay savouring this and wondering about the scent, which at first I couldn't place. Then it suddenly came to me: after-shave lotion! If, as I firmly believe, my dear husband had been allowed to contact me, he could have used nothing more evidential. He was an extremely down-to-earth man, not for him roses, lilies or violets. After-shave lotion would be his choice. So typical and so perfectly natural.'

Ruth offers another explanation as to why a relative should appear in a particular way: the person chooses a method that will be especially convincing for the person he or she wishes to contact.

Her husband made a third appearance, again visual. As in the first instance, Fred appeared to a third person. Ruth says:

'I was in church, one Sunday morning, feeling rather low. I had been involved in an extraordinary legal matter, not of my making, and was under great stress.

'During the singing of the hymn, about half-way through, I suddenly had an uplifting sense of great peace. After the service the vicar's wife invited me and a few others to the vicarage for coffee.

'As I was leaving a man I knew only slightly said to me, "I have something to tell you. Your husband was in church this morning. He was standing by your side during the hymn."

'I felt too overcome to speak but after I arrived home I telephoned this man and thanked him. He said: "There was a message for you too, that everything would be all right."

'And not long after it was.'

Was the man who saw him chosen because Fred knew he could be relied on not to doubt but simply to pass the message on?

And why didn't Fred approach Ruth directly? Did he perhaps feel in her troubled state that she needed some objective indication that it wasn't all in her mind?

It is often difficult to accept the role of messenger, especially if the message brings bad news. Elizabeth, who lives in Wales, found herself in such a dilemma. She recalls:

'In the spring of 1944 I had the clearest visual visit from my friend Donald, a lieutenant with a regiment who were defending Anzio. At about 7 a.m. I was awakened by my bedroom door opening. In walked Donald, who was then 24 years old. He was dressed in battle dress – in which I had never seen him before. His tin hat was awry and he was very white.

'He said: "I'm all right. Please will you tell Mary I am all right? Will you?"

' "Of course," I said, and he turned and left, shutting the door behind him.

'I concluded he had been wounded, perhaps in the head. I met his best friend Jeremy that day and told him what had happened and asked for Mary's telephone number. "For Heaven's sake, don't tell her – she's worried enough and you know you are imaginative," was Jeremy's response.

'So I didn't say any more, but each following day Donald was with me, saying, "You promised."

'Finally after four days I thought "To hell with Jeremy" and I rang Mary. I told her I thought Donald had been wounded. She was in fact very grateful I had telephoned. But within ten minutes she rang back. "I've just had a telegram, Liz. He was killed."

'I draw no deep conclusion from this except thankfulness that I had prepared her for the news in time. The date and time of his death were later verified by a friend and were those of Donald's first appearance.'

Such third-person links can confirm that spiritual ties in time of need may not spring from wishful thinking or natural anxiety. And it's not only married couples whose love can span the distance death creates. Josie's contact with her fiancé was direct and enduring. Indeed, she feels it was Derek's love and approval that sustained her throughout the years after his untimely death.

'The day before Derek, my fiancé, died in a motoring accident,' she told me, 'a little money spider suddenly spun down from my hair on a thread right over my nose. We laughed as we put it on the ground and it seemed a special symbol of our love.

'On the day of Derek's funeral I was managing well until we reached the cemetery. Then I became very upset, but at that moment a little money spider appeared again on a thread dangling below the end of my nose and a wonderful perfume and sense of knowing that everything was all right filled me. I was happy for Derek. Over the next couple of years the perfume would sometimes just appear, so overpowering I could almost touch the pure flower essence.

'Derek's parents lived on the other side of the world. I had never met them and we didn't keep in touch. But seven or eight years after Derek's death I became very agitated one evening and felt his presence very strongly. He had a message for his father. But how could I phone his parents to say I'd got a message from their dead son? At last the urge became so insistent I did ring them, at about midnight our time. It was as if his Dad was expecting me to call, though that sounds strange. I told him: "Derek says there's a small shed in the garden and a red bush in the middle. He says he is very close to you when you are by the red bush."

'I'd never seen the house of course, and Derek hadn't told me much about his home.

'Yet Derek's dad seemed to accept what I was saying quite naturally. Yes, he confirmed, the small shed had all Derek's things in and there was a red bush in the middle just as I had described. What is more, he had felt always felt his son very close when he stood by the red bush but he had dismissed it as wishful thinking. I believe the importance of any message is making things feel right to the person for whom it is intended. His dad accepted the message and it confirmed what he had been feeling, that Derek really was still there.

'As for the money spider, it appeared for a third time hanging above my nose from my hair as I stood in the church porch having my wedding photos taken, years later. I felt it set a sort of blessing on the marriage and that Derek was happy for me.'

The feeling that a deceased partner is blessing a second marriage must provide a wonderful sense of relief for the person left behind. But this is not always so, and the presence of a partner who has died may also cause real distress to a new husband or wife. It is important for someone who has been happily married before not to make the new partner feel second-best albeit unintentionally, as happened in the case of Emma who lives in the south of England.

'My husband's wife Penelope died four years ago. Two years later Graham and I decided to marry. We had always got on well together but having decided on marriage we began to have a series of petty quarrels. One afternoon we returned to his house in a disgruntled frame of mind.

'I was walking through the sitting room on my way to the kitchen. Halfway across the room I stopped and my way was blocked by a light or form of radiance that filled the space in front of me.

'Graham, who was behind me, gave me a push and said, "Go on".

'I went into the kitchen, put the kettle on to boil but couldn't settle. I went back into the sitting room but it was quite dark and now there was nothing. While I was standing feeling very bewildered Graham came into the room. He said quite calmly, "Penny's been here."

'I wish I could say that I was immediately filled with a sense of wonder. Quite the opposite. I became upset and caused a scene with the result that we were estranged for several months. But eventually we made up our quarrel. Just prior to our wedding the lady who lived in the flat upstairs from Graham told us of what had been a very frightening experience for her. Something filled the hall and stairway, she said, and at the same time there was a very strong smell of roses. My husband-to-be wasn't in the least surprised. "Oh my first wife Penny's around letting me know it's all right to marry Emma."

Some people might not feel threatened by such an experience, but remarriage is such a sensitive area and a first partner can so easily get sanctified that perhaps a realistic view of one's first wife or husband can be helpful. And a touch of humour never goes amiss.

Ivy is a lively 80-year-old from Kent whose full life has included two happy marriages that have extended beyond the grave.

'My dead husbands kept an eye on me for several years,' she told me. 'Indeed, both former spouses came back regularly to sit on my bed and vie for my attention. Contact with my first husband Ted started almost straight after his death. When he died he was a complete cripple and I felt his death as a merciful release, dearly though I loved him. I had chosen "Rock of Ages" as the hymn for his funeral service but I didn't tell anyone except the vicar.

'A medium friend rang up on the Sunday before the funeral and said, "I have a message from Ted. He says he thinks a lot of 'Rock of Ages' so he's glad you've picked it. Then she went on to tell me, "Oh, Ivy. I had the most wonderful experience this morning. I was sitting up in bed and the room was filled with a blue light and I saw a blue door and coming from the other side I heard your husband's voice saying proudly: 'I walked all by myself through the door and up all the stairs and on the other side there was the light. Now I can rest.' "

'A couple of months later, I saw Ted myself. It was wonderful. He looked like a young man again. He came and sat on the side of my bed. "Ted, how are you?" I asked him. "Marvellous. I walk everywhere because I haven't walked in so many years."

'A year later I married Ron from next door. I had helped nurse his wife through her last illness and he was very good to me when Ted was ill. We'd come together through sorrow and realized now we could be happy together.

'I'd only ever known Ron with white curly hair. I used to tease him and say, "I wish I could have seen you as you were when your hair was dark. I bet you were a smasher." Of course he still was a smasher but I never told him in case he got big-headed.

'When Ron died, some years later, he also started to come and visit me. One night I just saw his head and shoulders by the bed.

He was wearing his old Navy cap with a peak that he used to wear when he did his DIY jobs round the place.

'But Ron's face was different, much younger – he was 82 when he died. It was the face of the young Ron I could see. "Can I take your cap off?" I asked, knowing what he had come to show me. And there was his hair, dark and curly. He really was a smasher. And I told him so.'

'But didn't your dead husbands get jealous of each other?' I asked Ivy, thinking of the problems ex-husbands can present in everyday life as well as the very real distress Emma felt when confronted with her Graham's first wife.

'Oh, no,' smiled Ivy, 'Ron and Ted liked coming together, you see. They used to sit there side by side chatting away to me, though I have to admit they did compete a bit for my attention. In fact it was me suggested they should get together on the other side in the first place. They had been great friends when they were alive. We shared lots of memories so there was always plenty to talk about.

'But when I got married a third time, to Alf, my first two husbands stopped coming. To tell the truth, I started to feel a bit neglected. One night, Alf and I went along to a spiritualist church in Bromley. The medium said to me: "I've got two gentlemen here." She went on to describe Ted and Ron. "They say you're feeling a bit neglected."

'Alf looked surprised. Not exactly the message for a newlywed. I hadn't mentioned the visitations to him as it hadn't seemed tactful.

'The medium said: "They want to say they've been keeping away because they didn't want to muscle in now you've got your new husband and they are glad you don't need them any more."

Couples who've been together for most of their lives don't become separate entities overnight when one of the partners dies. Many elderly widows and widowers do continue to chat to their partners regularly. Perhaps it's only if the departed partner becomes more important than living people that those caring for the elderly person, whether family, friends or professional counsellors, need to see if there is enough earthly input in that person's life. If we can offer old people little in the way of fulfilment it's not surprising many prefer the past.

And hard though it is, when a widow or widower remarries, it's not realistic to expect him or her to wipe out a former marriage from memory and life. It's not disloyal to a new partner to recall the former happy times, though perhaps it's more tactful to do this with a third person.

If you want to feel close to a deceased partner, you can go to a favourite place and recall the happy times (and even smile through your tears). Or, if you want, you can get in touch with a reputable medium (see the Useful Addresses chapter of this book). Never, never dabble with Ouija boards or other spiritual paraphernalia you cannot control.

Darryl was killed in a motor-bike crash when he was 16. Six months later his girlfriend was persuaded to join in a Ouija board session. Sure enough Darryl came through with names and dates. Then Sian asked if he had really loved her. The glass spelled out terrible obscenities and told her he had never been faithful. Then the glass went wild and smashed. Malicious friends pushing the glass for a sick joke? Or it might have been some malicious spirit who had taken over the line of communication.

Naturally Sian was heartbroken but felt unable to confide in anyone. Then dark shadows started to appear round her bed and whisperings that went on and off through the years until at last she contacted a spiritual healer who helped her to devise a way to banish the menacing presences from her life. Though she is married now she still regrets bitterly agreeing to the seance. Darryl was very important to her but the seeds of doubt were sown that soured several future relationships.

If you have lost a partner or even a close friend, just reach out directly and feel the love that surrounds you and know death does not part those whom love joins.

6

I Just Called to Say I Love You

Why should our dead relatives return at all? Perhaps because the bonds of family are not for this lifetime only. And, just as in life parents will phone just to say 'hello' or send loving thoughts, so too the most touching and frequent 'calls from beyond' are simply to express love and to share everyday concerns between parent and adult child.

Sharon's father died suddenly after suffering a heart attack. The night before his funeral she had a vivid dream. 'I dreamed I had a phone call from Dad. He said: "I just called to say I love you and to say goodbye."

'I tried to reach him as I could see his face, but he was in a long dark tunnel with a bright light round it and was going further and further away from me.'

The story went on for Sharon, a mother herself who lives in the Home Counties. She told me: 'Early one morning I had to ring my mum and a man who sounded just like Dad answered the phone and said: "Hello Sharon, love, what's wrong?"

' "Who's that?" I asked.

' "Why it's Dad of course. Who else would it be?"

'I put down the phone and dialled again straight away. Mum answered. She'd gone to the phone when it rang but no one was there.'

Sharon's was not the only contact with her deceased father. 'The night before my dad's funeral, Mum was lying half-awake on the bed when she saw my dad's mum, who had died nearly 26 years earlier. Her mother-in-law sat on the end of the bed looking at her and said, "He's all right, Gwen, he's in no pain," and then she disappeared.

'Then a couple of months later Mum and my sister went to

Spain for a rest. My sister woke in the early hours and saw someone sitting on the end of Mum's bed. It didn't look like Mum but she thought it was just a trick of the light and that Mum must have been unable to sleep. She asked her what was wrong and the figure disappeared. She realized Mum was fast asleep in the bed next to her all the time. In the morning she described the figure and Mum said it was Dad's mum, whom my sister and I had never met because she'd died before we were born. But why should Dad's mum be the one to watch over Mum, and not Dad? Why should I have seen Dad when Mum hasn't?

Sharon's experience would seem to tie in with one churchman's ideas of the 'good dead', the spirits who come back to keep an eye on us or, as Sharon's dad put it, just to call to say 'I love you.'

The Reverend Tom Willis of the Church of England believes that such contact can be positive. As well as being parish priest for Sewerby, near Bridlington, he has responsibility for dealing with the darker side of the paranormal for the diocese of York. He is an officially appointed exorcist and has lectured and appeared on radio and television to talk on the subject. He has been married for 30 years, has five children and is a man of great humour and compassion. While he believes in what he calls 'the good dead' he doesn't hesitate to call a demon a demon.

'The good dead, as I call them, may well be just deceased family popping in to see if everything is all right. Recently I was lecturing to a women's group in Scarborough and a young woman there told me that her father-in-law had been staying with her and her husband. One morning she'd asked him to go upstairs to put some socks and handkerchiefs away in the drawers. When he came back down he was as white as a sheet.

' "What's wrong?" the young woman asked.

' "I put the socks and hankies away as you said," he replied, "and when I turned round there was my dead father standing in front of me. 'Hello son,' he said."

'Her father-in-law didn't know what to say to this. "I just came to see how you all are," his father went on.

'Still her father-in-law couldn't speak. "I'm sorry, I'm frightening you," his father said, "I'll go."

'And that's how it is with families. Occasionally the good dead will visit but they don't normally let themselves be seen. It's as if they suddenly realize, "Whoops, you can see me!" and off they go because the good dead don't want to frighten us.

'I hear the same thing again and again. One in ten people out of any group will have seen a ghost and now and again it's fine and just part of the loving process. Lots of people report they will suddenly smell their mother's perfume or dad's tobacco while watching telly. And that's the lightest form of contact from beyond, the least disturbing because it brings fond memories back.

'Of course psychiatrists and psychologists will say it's just your mind creating these things, but it happens at times when people say they weren't even thinking of the person. Or they will feel a hand on their shoulder, or be in the garden and see a shadow.'

Many of the routine contacts from beyond recall an old family saying or joke. Since many of these experiences do come via a medium or third person, they can reassure us it's not all imagination, for the other person knows nothing about the family pet name you were given at three months old (and would sooner forget!).

Over the years I have been told numerous such examples of messages that have meant something only to the person who received them. Let me recount a few of them.

Elise, an accountant in the south of England, was talking to a woman who turned out to be a medium. 'Does the phrase "dog bites pig" mean anything to you?' the woman asked. It didn't, so the medium suggested Elise asked her mother. Her mother was equally puzzled until she remembered her gran used to say it when she was a very little girl. She'd say it when her grandad would bring home a particular friend whom gran didn't approve of who had a pig-like face. The men used to argue and grandad used to get so angry he growled. Gran used to mutter, 'dog bites pig'. Elise's mother had forgotten the incident and had certainly never told Elise.

Joe's dad loved clotted cream and on retirement he and his wife moved to Cornwall. So great was his love of the local delicacy that whenever any of the family came to stay he would insist on driving miles round the winding lanes so they could end every outing at a teashop. Joe told me: 'The week after the old man's funeral, the family were still in Cornwall and it was boiling hot. One day we ran out of sun oil, so rubbed cream into our skin instead. "How Dad would have laughed," someone said.

'Months later I had occasion to go to a spiritualist church in Wiltshire. I have only been three times in my whole life and I'm 80 now. The medium pointed to me and said, "I can see a dish of clotted cream being held out to me. I hope it makes sense to you." '

Just before Kath's dad died he had gone on holiday with the family. The high point of the holiday was when Kath's little girl Lizzie had taken a ride on a very undersized donkey who almost buckled under her weight. Kath's dad had laughed till he cried.

Many years later Kath went to a spiritualist church. The medium told her that her dad was there. 'I really thought she was going to break that donkey's back,' was the message.

I could go on forever with such stories. One good thing about the personal nature of these messages is that they thwart the scourge of spiritualist churches – the professional 'message-claimers' – those people who sit in the audience believing that every spirit who comes through the medium must be a relation of theirs.

At one meeting I went to there was an elderly lady who claimed six entities in under an hour. But that particular medium had problems anyway. At one point he had eight members claiming the same sailor. In such a situation how can you tell if the message coming through is for you or not? Listen carefully for the inevitable snippets that could only apply to you. Whether they are acknowledged as yours is irrelevant. You are not taking part in a psychic bingo session where a prize is given to the person with the most number of messages claimed on their card at the end of the session. If you are there it is to receive a very private communication; as long as *you* know what the message means, that is enough.

You will know it because of some giveaway phrase. Even if you can claim it and get a chance to quiz the medium you may not get a lot more information. How or why contact is made we don't know. And when you think about it, we are asking an awful lot of any medium to produce to order at a set time and given place contact with a specific set of relatives beyond. When they fail we are all too ready to dismiss the whole concept as rubbish and the medium as a fake.

The Reverend Willis does suggest caution in accepting third-person contact lock, stock and barrel. While he's happy to accept that if Gran actually materializes in front of you, it probably is her, he does point out that you need to take a bit more care with less direct forms of contact. 'Something pretending to be a relative might come instead,' he told me. 'It's amazingly easy to be fooled. Let me give you an example. It's like talking on the telephone. My wife's father was adamant that it wasn't possible to mistake Anne's voice for her mother's, though other people had. One day Dad rang up and Anne answered but he thought it was his wife. Anne strung him along, asking how his day at the office was, etc. If such mistakes can happen over the phone with the people closest to you, how much more possible is it for something from beyond to fool you? You're talking to someone you cannot see and it can cause great trouble.'

So how can you be sure it really is Mum or Dad sending the message? You're on fairly safe ground if the messages talk about the ordinary day-to-day stuff that is only of interest to you and that person. After all, the average family conversation (outside the more glamorous soap operas) would have the average listener snoring within seconds. Contact with close relatives beyond is rather like the kind of long-distance phone call you get from a call box, full of 'have you?' and 'you haven't!' with a bit of love slipped in before the money runs out.

Occasionally such third-party personalized messages from beyond can be disturbing though they are sent with loving intent.

Alice is in her late forties and had never been to a spiritualist gathering before. Indeed, she had only gone along to the group because a friend persuaded her to keep her company.

'The medium didn't know me from Adam. I think it was the first time she had been to our town. I couldn't believe it when she picked on me and told me she'd got an older man in a trilby hat and a grey suit. My dad, who had died 20 years before, used to wear a grey suit and trilby to go to work. But then lots of older men did. "He's laughing and singing 'Polly Put The Kettle On'. I can't make head nor tail of it," the medium said.

'I could. Our next door neighbour when I was a kid was called Polly and Dad used to drive us mad singing or whistling 'Polly Put the Kettle On' every time we saw her. I can see him now doing it, in his old grey suit and trilby when he got home from work.'

'I bet you were pleased,' I said to Alice.

'Pleased? I fled for my life there and then and I've never gone near a spiritualist meeting since.'

As I said, messages from mediums may not be the way you want to be in contact with deceased members of your family. Alice can smile now, but for many people continuing love is a very private thing and you may find it more upsetting than you can imagine to receive a loving message, especially if it is the first contact, in a public place.

Annette, who lives in Leicestershire, also had this problem. She told me:

'I went to see Doris Stokes in April, 1984. I know she is the butt of a lot of jokes but this night she really was spot on. She kept going on about October and the 26th, Charles Street, an Edie and someone going to Australia. I was too nervous to respond and regretted it bitterly. Both my grandfathers died within two weeks of each other. One died on 26th October and his sister – my Aunty Deborah – was about to go to Australia. The other grandfather had lived in Charles Street and had a wife called Edie. My sister was with me and afterwards we could not believe that we had not responded. I do wish I had taken it further.'

Relatives can be remarkably persistent and since they couldn't contact Annette through a medium, next time her departed nearest and dearest tried the direct approach. No less than Aunty Deborah herself. Annette recalls: 'The only person I believe I have ever seen is my Aunty Deborah. I was not thinking of her at that particular moment – in fact I was dishing up the children's dinner. The oldest three were sitting at the table in the dining room with the youngest two in the kitchen with me. The serving hatch was open and as I went to it to pass food through I looked beyond the table and saw Aunty Deborah standing there. She was wearing a favourite cardigan which I had seen her in many times. The vision only lasted a few seconds. I felt quite calm afterwards and not at all worried that she would appear and frighten me. I have never seen her again. It was a couple of days before the first anniversary of her death.

'Aunty Deborah and I weren't particularly close, although she was very close to my mother as she helped to bring her up in early childhood. However I believe I am temperamentally quite like her and can often identify my feelings with her behaviour. My mother occasionally remarks I am behaving "like Aunty Deborah" or that I have my "Aunty Deborah face" on.'

Spiritualism is one way of getting reassurance that life goes on after death, but it is to be taken very seriously. You may go to a spiritualist church or mediumistic demonstration and not get a message or, like Alice and Annette, find it too overwhelming. The churches aren't in the least frightening or spooky; spiritualists are for the most part friendly, compassionate and down-to-earth folk. But if you do want to go along, ring up in advance and see if you can have a chat with someone to explain it all to you and reassure you. The Reverend Willis has his own doubts about relying on spiritualism, as I have mentioned. 'People want to know that a deceased relative is still alive – so it's natural enough they may want to go along to a spiritualist church or medium,' he told me. 'But when they keep going and getting advice they must act on – e.g. a husband says you must invest your savings, etc. – then the worry of being controlled from beyond creeps in. We assume the dead must know more than we do. They know what it is like to be dead, but they don't necessarily know what's going on here. Otherwise they wouldn't need to pop in to see how things were. Their advice may be no better than it was when they were on earth.'

The other side of the coin is shown by Susan of Manchester, who told me: 'I do not believe in contacting the dead. I believe they should be left in peace. However, it does seem to me that sometimes they do not leave *us* in peace. They do seem to want to contact us. The story involving my late mother is one of comfort and reassurance.'

'My mother was a very sensible, down-to earth sort of person who would have no truck with any aspect of the supernatural. We could not even tell her when we had a bad dream. We are a small, very close family. Mother died at almost 90 after a short illness. My sisters and I were sad but not overcome with grief – but I knew that the funeral was going to be hard for me.

'As I walked behind the coffin in the cemetery I felt as though there was a great weight pressing my head downwards so I could not lift it to look up. While the coffin was being lowered into the ground I heard my mother's voice in my ear – not in my head, it was in my ear – and she said, "I just want to rest."

'She had said exactly this a number of times in the last few weeks of her life and so it seemed natural to hear her say it then.

'On hearing her voice the weight lifted from my head and I was able to look up at the bright blue, clear December sky. There were two white birds just above us. I thought to myself, "Someone has come for her." After the funeral I remarked to my sisters about what I had heard. The sister standing next to me at the funeral said that she had heard the words too. Strangely, a year or so later my sister had no memory of this and in fact hardly recalled the funeral at all. Perhaps she just did not want to remember an unhappy time. But we all agree that we feel mother hovering quite often and we talk to her. We find ourselves turning into her in our words and expressions.'

Familiar sounds can be one way for the dead to contact us. Gemma lost her brother during the Falklands War. On the anniversary of his death she and her husband were sitting downstairs when suddenly they heard someone walking along their upstairs hall. Her husband rushed upstairs but there was nothing to be seen. The footsteps were just like the sound Gemma's brother used to make thudding about in his heavy army boots. Gemma feels sure it was her brother saying goodbye. She never heard the sound again.

Messages and messengers come in all shapes and forms. Megan is a district nurse and finds that working so closely with sick people can make her receptive to all kinds of unseen forces. She has learned to keep quiet about what she sees, but one day the urge to tell the person she was with was overwhelming.

'I had a student on my round with me one week. She was very competent and helpful but I couldn't settle to work.

'I saw in front of her a farmhouse kitchen with lots of pots of honey and a woman who looked like the student but older and a girl of about nine helping her. It was ridiculous because we were in the centre of Birmingham. I tried to forget it but the picture stayed there so I mentioned the scene as nonchalantly as I could.

'The girl burst into tears. "If I tell you I can see a bedroom with a high chest of drawers and a string of pearls, does that make sense?" I asked her. I wished I'd never said anything.

' "I will be 21 in a fortnight," she told me, just about managing a smile. "My mother is dead. We lived in a farmhouse in Staffordshire and my mother kept bees. I used to help her label the honey pots in the kitchen. She died when I was about nine. People say I look like her when she was young."

' "It's funny you should see her now, because I have been missing her dreadfully lately and I'm due to get the pearls on my twenty-first birthday."

'I could see a large stool that had been upholstered by hand with a lovely tapestry design. When I told the student, she said, "My mother did that. Tapestry work was her hobby."

'It was the first time she had ever been in touch with her mum, though she had been thinking about her all week for some reason. But after that whenever she thought of her mother, the pain was gone and she felt her close.'

Sometimes contact may be so subtle we almost doubt it is more than imagination, yet such encounters may be the most reassuring and least frightening of all. And it may be that those we love do know best how we would welcome their return and certainly have no intention of frightening us. A sense of the dead person or his or her favourite scent can be as reassuring as seeing the person. Elspeth is a solicitor working on the south coast. Her psychic link with her father began when she was quite young.

'When Dad died, he had his Guinness on his left and his dog on his right, smoothing his fur. He was laughing and joking to his last breath. "Dad, stop mucking about," I said and then I caught his hand as I realized. "Dad, I love you," I said, and I know he heard me.

'I phoned my son Martin. I just said, "Can you come round?"

'Before I said more, he said, "On my way."

'As I opened the door to him, he said, "How long ago did Grandad go?"

'I hadn't needed to tell him though it was so unexpected. "How did you know?" I asked, but it was a silly question. "Oh, I found myself saying 'Bye, Grandad,' for no reason a few minutes ago, so I thought he must have died."

'Martin and I were both criticized because at the funeral neither of us cried. "It's the shock," the family said. "Better keep an eye on her," as though I had suddenly gone simple.

'I didn't even try to explain. If they didn't know Dad was still there, they never would.

'I sold the house where Dad and I lived in 1988 because it was too big for me on my own and moved to a bungalow that was built the same year I was born. To my intense pleasure Dad followed me there. Dad always used to smoke Clan tobacco. As he got older he suffered from rheumatism and would rub in muscle relaxing cream to help. Quite often, especially in the evenings, I smell Dad's tobacco and the cream in the bungalow.

'It might seem strange as Dad never lived there, but if someone loves you during their lifetime that relationship can't just finish on earth. They still look after you when they are gone. My son is 32 and has always shared a psychic bond with me, as he did with my dad.

'The first time my son realized Dad was around was a few months after Dad's death, not long after I'd moved. Martin walked in with his wife, stopped in his tracks, sniffed and grinned. "Visitors?" he asked and I knew he could smell dad's tobacco and cream. Now whenever he comes over he says, "Hi, Grandad," as he walks in.

'But it's not surprising Dad communicates with me. He had experience himself of the psychic link after death even before I was born. Dad was working for a tug company in Southampton at the time and his younger brother was seriously ill. Dad was walking along the quay with another man when he saw his brother walking on his left-hand side. "Look, Eddie," his brother said, "I'm sorry about this, but I'm too tired to go on so I came to say cheerio." "I know, George," Dad replied, "I'll see you again."

'The chap who was with Dad said, "Whom are you talking to?" "Oh, just myself," Dad replied.

'He drove straight home and Mum was waiting to tell him there had been phone call from the hospital. "I know," Dad said, "George has died."

'I believe there are only certain people in this world who have the capacity to see beyond this life. Or perhaps we all have it but are afraid to allow ourselves to communicate in this way. Some people would be terrified if a dead relative turned up. So the person won't appear if he knows it would frighten you. A parent wouldn't want to upset a child by appearing. Dad wouldn't be around my house if it frightened me. A person doesn't change when he dies.'

As well as these 'everyday' encounters, a dead parent may return particularly to comfort an adult child at a difficult period in his or her life. The desire for kindly parental wisdom and support is so strong that sometimes it seems they can still hear and respond to your cry. Janet, a single parent living with her two children in the Home Counties, told me:

'Six months before I split up from my husband, when things were going very wrong in my life, I saw my dad. It was five or six years after he died. After my mother had died I had always felt her around but never my dad. When Dad came to me it seemed as though I was out of my body. Some people might dismiss what happened as a very vivid dream but it was more than that, I'm sure.

'I saw a light in the living room. The chair was in a different place and as I came downstairs Mum was sitting there. "Hello, Mum," I said, "how are you?"

' "How are you?" she asked. "I was worried so I've brought someone to see you."

'I turned round and there was my dad sitting in the armchair. "Hello, love," he said. "You can touch me if you like. I'm real."

'I held his hand and he seemed to read my thoughts. "I'm not a figment of your imagination," he told me.

'And then I found myself back in bed. But it was a wonderful experience and helped me to get through a difficult patch.'

How then can you contact your departed relative safely to convey your continuing love and need of them? Some people do find a private session with a reliable medium helpful (see the Useful Addresses chapter of this book for reputable organizations that will put you in touch with help that won't fleece you). Others may find a spiritualist church a way of affirming that families do go on. I have met many wonderful and eminently sensible mediums who do a lot of good for the bereaved.

For other people a formal approach to the deceased family seems artificial and too deliberate. At the end of the day you know best for yourself. If you want to reach out personally and privately to a dead parent or partner, you will feel directly the peace and caring that can never die. The link of love – in life or death – needs no formal training.

As for the rest – psychic fairs with rows of clairvoyants are *not* the place to explore personal relationships with the dead. Ten or more appointments in a day in an atmosphere where money is changing hands like the first day at the sales is not in my opinion a place to discover anything but the depth of your purse.

'I just called to say I love you' is a welcoming message at any time. From those we have loved and lost it may be especially reassuring at those times when we feel sad or alone and only Mum or Dad will do. Remember, too, the present day. It may be difficult at times, when very much alive relatives can sometimes be awkward, to look beyond the immediate and express the underlying love. Sentimental though it seems, why not ring mum up right now and say 'I just called to tell you I love you.' Families are for now as well as forever.

7

Guardian Angels

Some deceased relatives adopt a 'guardian angel' role towards the family they have left behind. This is often rooted in a particularly strong bond that existed between two family members in life.

Alison was alone in the exercise yard of her local riding school. A sudden sound caused her horse to panic. He knocked her to the ground and reared over her. Then Alison heard her grandmother, who had been dead for five years say: 'Roll towards my voice, Ally.'

Alison was stunned and didn't respond. The voice became more and more insistent until she moved towards the sound of her grandmother's voice – just at the moment the horse's hooves came crashing towards her head. She escaped with lacerations.

Grandmother had proved a lifesaver in death – just as she had often helped Alison in life. The late medium George Finn, who lived in Dorset, also had reason to thank his grandmother for saving his life. George was a member of the Airborne Gliders during the Second World War and was taken prisoner by the Germans. He and one of his companions were taken to separate rooms and interrogated about another Airborne division and one man in particular reportedly running operations. But the Germans had been misinformed: at the time no such division existed, although they refused to believe this. If George refused to hand over the name he would be executed. But he had no name to give, so his only chance was to lie. However, his lie would be checked. In the next room the other soldier was also being interrogated. He too would have to lie to save his life, but if his lie was different from George's then they would both be killed.

Their lives now hung on the million-to-one chance that they would independently choose the same name.

In such a situation there is no help in this world, so George turned to the next one. At the time George was not involved in spiritualism but he remembered that his grandmother had told him when she died that if ever he was in trouble he had only to ask and she would come and help him.

'Help, Gran,' he asked silently.

The name Evans came into his head and he told the interrogators that was the name of the man leading the operations. They said that if his friend gave the same name he would be spared.

Out of nowhere the name Evans came to the man in the next room. Both their lives were spared.

Had Gran come back in person to whisper a name to George and his friend, or had the belief in her power enabled George to practise telepathy? The result was the same. Whether our own inner powers are being triggered or the help comes from beyond – or a mixture of both – love can fuel a rescue.

Fathers, too, can protect their young in times of fear or danger. Phyllis from Surrey was reassured by her dead father that if she stayed put she would be safe during an air raid in the Second World War.

'It was about two in the morning and my daughter and I were in the shelter. My husband was away fire-watching. There was a very bad raid going on and a bomb was dropped quite near to us. I threw my little girl on the floor and put myself on top of her and stayed there for ages. When things were quieter I put my daughter back in her bunk and sat on the edge of mine wondering whether it was safe to leave the shelter yet.

'Presently I heard the garden gate click. Wondering who it could be I looked out. It was a beautiful summer's day. The sun was shining and the birds were singing and there was my dead father coming towards me. He said: "You will both be quite all right if you stay in here. How cosy you have made it. I am going down

78

the garden to look at your new pond." With that he went and it was dark again.'

Coincidence or a helping hand from beyond? Of course there is no proof in such cases. But an abiding sense that we are cared for can trigger our own inner resources to action so we can access information that can keep us safe.

Francis, who lives on the south coast of England, told me:

'My father promised me when he was very ill, "I'll come back and let you know I am all right, so don't worry or grieve." '

Later he saw a vision of his father in which the old man looked wonderful. Francis found this reassuring enough, but his father continued to return with practical advice when his son was in difficulty or likely to make a serious mistake.

'Once I was about to go into business with someone I liked but didn't know very well. I would have invested everything and, however you looked at it, the deal seemed sound. But the night before I was due to sign the papers my dad came to tell me not to. As he'd never given me bad advice I knew I must take him seriously and I'm glad I did. If I hadn't listened it would have been an utter disaster because I later found out that the man had previous business debts. How can a dead man warn me of something I didn't know myself? I can't explain in rational terms but I know my dad is with me and will always help me just as he used to when he was alive. I've left my body a few times and gone to this wonderful place that is so – serene is the word. If death's like that I don't mind dying.'

Fathers from beyond need not make direct contact with their offspring to show that they are still taking an interest in the affairs of the living. One example was given by Ralph, who lives in Brisbane, Australia.

'I won a scholarship to study pharmacy. In early 1936, my late father came to my mother shortly before some important exams I was due to take and warned her that I wouldn't qualify but that all would be well, she wasn't to worry.

'My mother naturally didn't tell me at the time but she told a colleague at work that she was worried something dreadful would happen to me to prevent my passing the exams as I was doing well and on a sure course for success. For she never doubted my father's words.

'Since I had won several prizes during the year I had absolutely no qualms about the exams. After feeling confident that I had done well in the written exams I had three weeks' wait before the five days of practicals. But after two weeks I began to vomit. The doctor said it was "examination colic" but my mother was certain I had appendicitis because of the warning. Of course she was right so I was rushed to hospital the following day with a gangrenous appendix bordering on peritonitis.

'It was the last chance to sit the botany exam and I could not afford to spend another two years studying the new syllabus.

'But, as my father had said, all was well in the end. I recovered rapidly and went on to take a doctorate in biochemistry. And there was another positive by-product of the experience. As a result of my mother's experience, her colleague, who had lost his wife the previous year, felt that death was not the end.'

So in this case Ralph's late father not only helped his wife and son but also a third party who was not lucky enough to have direct contact of his own – so far as we know.

Nor was this Ralph's father's first contact with his wife, though it was the most direct. Indeed, he had prepared her for the bad news of his death, as Ralph explains:

'Early in February, 1919, in the week my father was due to return from France where he had been guarding German prisoners of war, my mother had the same extremely vivid dream three times. She dreamed that my father returned in his army clothes, changed, got on his bicycle and rode down the main road of the town. In the sky were the words, "Missing, missing, missing".

'The next morning her father-in-law came to the door with the message that my father had died suddenly from bronchial pneumonia. The message should have come direct to my mother but in error my grandfather had been informed first.'

Sometimes, however, the advice of a guardian goes ignored or cannot be interpreted. If grandfather had been listened to, then perhaps Rosanne would have found her stolen car far more quickly. Grandfather was the invisible friend of three-year-old Nicklas, as his mother Rosanne told me.

'One Saturday I woke up in the early hours screaming. I had dreamed that my father was dead. My father was a healthy 65-year-old who'd never been really ill in his life. On the Monday I had a phone call to say my dad had died of a heart attack. Nicklas and my dad had been very close even though Nicklas was only three. I was pregnant with my daughter Karen when my dad died.

'When Nicklas was about four he started talking about his grandad who "lives in the sky". Then when he started school he would write about his grandad so I realized Nicklas still thought about him a great deal.

'When Nicklas was six he started to talk about his "guard" and said that Grandad lived inside him now and talked to him. Sometimes he would go into a corner and start talking to Grandad or his guard – who seemed to be one and the same and who acted as his guardian angel.

'Then our car was stolen. It had belonged to my dad. The following afternoon Nicklas came to me in the garden and said that his guard knew where the car was.

'Nicklas kept going across the lawn and apparently talking into thin air, listening and then coming back to me. He said there were two bridges and the car was by the first bridge. There were a lot of shops not far away and sometimes we went to the place for a picnic and there was a special church I had been to. He insisted I knew where the church was. When I suggested several places Nicklas got annoyed and said it was where cars went over and under the bridges. I was stumped and put it down to an overactive imagination.

'When the car was found it was on a slip road just off a dual carriageway. There were two bridges nearby. The car was by the first bridge. A couple of miles back was Telford Shopping Centre and park, where we had had a couple of picnics, and not far to the right of the place was the spiritualist church that I had attended a couple of times since my father had died. A special church indeed, but how did Nicklas know?'

There are so many inexplicable strands in these, especially where children are involved, that it is hard to get to the truth of the matter. But it is important to accept what children say even if we cannot see or hear what they do.

But of course not everyone, not even another child, is always understanding about psychic experiences and this can cause great distress to a sensitive child. Samantha never knew her nan but she believed that her grandmother protected her from the things that frightened her at night.

'It began with two tall shining beings who used to stand in Samantha's room,' Samantha's mother June told me, 'but then she would see a tall woman who told her she had died in a fire in a flat. She also had other frightening visions and it was hard to reassure her she was safe.

'But Sam found her own solution. She started to chat to her nan every night and that stopped her feeling afraid of anything malevolent, for her nan was with her and would drive them away.

'It wasn't all imagination, whatever people might say. Samantha described things about my mother she couldn't possibly have known. She'd never met her yet she knew of her mannerisms and other little details I'd forgotten. Samantha's nightly chats with Nanny went on for two or three years or more, from when she was about seven.

'There was no problem at home since the contact made her happy and served such a positive purpose in her life and we are very open to such things in our household. But then Samantha mentioned her experiences at school and that made a lot of trouble for her since even children she knew who admitted privately they had seen similar visions themselves made fun of her and used Samantha to divert attention from their own experience. She had a really hard time and now won't talk about seeing her nan anymore.'

If there is one area that relatives – living or dead – are sure to have something to say about it is the choice of partner for a beloved child. A parent or favourite uncle from beyond is not above a bit of match-making.

'I went along to a spiritualist church one Sunday afternoon,' says Rachel of Birmingham. 'The medium asked me, "Do you know a tall, very well-built man called Big Henry?" "No," I replied, "but I wish I did."

'I could see the chap she was describing, blonde and rather nice with his hair falling forward.

'When I got home the phone rang. It was a man I knew very vaguely from work called Hal. "I'm sorry to trouble you on a Sunday afternoon," he said, "but I fell asleep and when I woke I saw my uncle who died when I was a boy. It was really strange."

' "Was he called Big Henry?" I asked.

' "How did you know that?" Hal said.

' "Did he have blonde hair pushed forward?"

' "Yes. But it doesn't make sense because he died when I was eight. I remember I had an appendix operation and dreamed about him and shortly afterwards he died unexpectedly. But I don't know why I should have seen him this afternoon or why I am phoning you now."

'It may have been a strange line in chat-ups, but Hal and I enjoyed a very nice friendship thanks to Big Henry.'

As in life, more often than not relatives are quick to show their disapproval of a partner. Joanne, who lives in Portsmouth, recalls:

'In her lifetime my great-gran was a working clairvoyant and had some very rare nineteenth-century astrology books. I would pore over them when I was nine or ten. They were so beautiful. One had a very distinctive frontispiece that was etched into my consciousness.

'In my older teens I had a particular boyfriend of whom I suspected my late great-gran wouldn't have approved. One day my boyfriend and I were walking along together when over a high garden wall I saw a very unusual old-fashioned yellow rose, Great-

Nan's favourite, and I suddenly thought of her. At that precise moment my boyfriend for some reason pointed to a piece of rolled-up paper in the road. I picked it up and when I unrolled it I saw it was the frontispiece of a copy of Great-Nan's rare nineteenth-century astrology book, complete with the name of the book and distinctive colouring. I just knew it was Great-Nan's way of saying the boy wasn't for me but I wasn't in any mood to listen to advice from anyone, living or dead.

'But Great-Nan wouldn't let it be. I went to college and in my room was a picture of the Black Madonna I'd brought back from holiday for her not long before her death. I was still mooning about this same boy and one morning sitting on the bed I said to myself "If I think about him hard enough I can make him come round to see me." I was really desperate to see him. At that moment the picture fell off the wall and crashed on to my bed next to me. Again I knew it was Great-Nan's way of warning me, saying I was being stupid, but I ignored the signs and the boy did end up causing me a great deal of distress. I wish I'd heeded my Great-Nan's warnings!'

Wise words from an unexpected quarter came to Hilda's daughter. Hilda explained:

'A few years ago my daughter was in difficulties with her marriage. She and her husband had gone off to Wales and hadn't got any money behind them. Her husband wasn't interested in keeping a job and they finally split up. She was alone with her young daughter to care for in a strange place and all seemed black. She could see no hope for the future and one night, after a particularly bad day, she went to sleep crying.

'During the night she woke up to find my mother standing by the side of her bed. Gran was dressed in her favourite red cardigan that she only wore for special occasions. She told my daughter to dry her tears and get on with making a new life for herself and her daughter and everything would turn out fine. My daughter took her gran's advice and after her divorce came back to live in Manchester, where she met her present husband. She now has a good job and is very happy. True and wise words from the other side – yet my mother never took much notice of my daughter when she was here with us. Perhaps she felt she was paying a debt that she felt she owed to the granddaughter she hadn't bothered with. Who knows?'

It may not be just one side of the family that takes against an 'unsuitable paramour'. Arthur got more than he bargained for at the local spiritualist church as he sat next to Vera, a very nice middle-aged divorcee in whom he had more than a friendly interest – unbeknownst to his wife. It may seem an unusual atmosphere for illicit passions, but then it's a fairly innocent venue for an errant husband to tell his wife he's visiting. After all, no wife is going to think that hubby will get up to anything there. Arthur was confident that everything was secret when the medium, who had never been to the church before, homed straight in on Arthur. She told Arthur that someone who was a relative of 'a close friend' wanted a word. She described in detail a formidable old lady who was not at all happy with the current situation.

'The grass is always greener on the other side of the fence, so be very careful before rushing off to pastures new or you might end up flat on your face,' was the warning.

In hurried whispers over the tea and buns, Vera explained to Arthur who the mystery visitor was. It was a very strait-laced old aunty of Vera's who disapproved of dalliance of any kind, much less involving extra-marital activities. That night Vera went to bed with a good book rather than Arthur.

If you are lucky enough to be protected in times of danger or even folly by a fond relative, then be glad and don't waste time worrying about the metaphysics of it all. On the down-side, be prepared for unwelcome advice that you may prefer not to hear – Uncle Jim may well speak his mind no more subtly than he used to in the Flying Horse on a Friday night.

So why aren't we all protected by our departed relatives? Perhaps we are and just don't recognize the source or even that we are being actively steered from a potentially hazardous path, the near-miss accident, the delay that stops us catching the bus that breaks down. In any case, we mustn't rely on guardians to bail us out. Support can be a welcome bonus to our earthly endeavours – but it's not a good idea to depend on the help and advice of others, living or dead. If you make your own decisions and consciously avoid life's pitfalls, then you may be pleasantly surprised to find you glimpse momentarily a shadowy figure or patch of light out of the corner of your eye. Is it wishful thinking or the extension of a family tie? For all of us who have experienced such protection, there can be little doubt that it exists, forever.

8

Unfinished Business

Love is perhaps then the main reason for departed family members to return. But almost as strong a motive is the nagging sense that there is still something to do back on earth. Unfinished business – the unpaid bill, the arrangements that weren't finalized, practical matters that left unresolved can cause so much heartache – can keep us awake at night. How much more so for the departed, who can't add their signature, change a decision or even paste up that final piece of wallpaper?

I met Richard, a New Zealand farmer, at his sister-in-law's home in Berkshire. He told me how his deceased father crossed the world to come to him.

'It was a spiritual link-up, yet the experience was almost tangible,' Richard told me.

'My father died in September, 1984, in England. I was living in New Zealand at the time. I was not close to my father. We had a difficult relationship when I was a child and only a distant connection when I became an adult.

'About two years after his death I was up early one Saturday. I was suddenly aware of my father in the room. I saw him so clearly. He was wearing his old jacket with the pockets full of odds and ends, his tobacco, notebook and biro pen (he always took down information he read in books). He had on a rather badly tied tie. I had a great sense that he was pleased with me. It was a heartwarming experience. During life he had not always been pleased with me, though when I was an adult we had a civilized relationship and he was proud of me on occasions and said so. Now he said, "It is not as I intended". Those were his only words.

'I was convinced he was talking about his Will, which had

87

caused many problems since his death. Though the wrongs couldn't be righted at least I understood he hadn't acted out of malice but through lack of foresight. After a while the experience ended and I was left with a lovely feeling towards my father, a feeling that he approved of me at last, like a blessing that set a seal on our relationship. I didn't say anything to him. I was just conscious of enjoying his presence as with a friend you have known for a long time. My father's words were peripheral to the experience. It was warm, positive and uplifting.'

Richard's experience was enriching and undid many of the old hurts as well as resolving the motives concerning the old man's property. Often it is this kind of unfinished business with the dead that can keep us from getting on with our own lives.

Anger at an unacknowledged injustice is the one thing that may keep a spirit pursuing a vendetta. A person who dies without being able to tell his side of the story may simply need the true situation acknowledged so that he may rest.

The message from beyond made no sense to Laura, a widow living in a south London suburb. She had been to a spiritualist church where the medium had received a message about a tin box. No one claimed it, which was unusual – cynics would say that a tin box is bound to mean something to someone so it's a safe bet to conjure one up if the evening's not going well. But Laura couldn't get the box out of her mind. She even mentioned it to her son Les.

To her surprise Les didn't scoff but immediately connected it with the tin box in which his late father used to collect subscriptions for a friendly society which his union ran at work. The money was kept in a tin box but the accounts were kept in Laura's late husband's head.

'My Dad was very honest and very trusting,' says Les. 'Often he'd let people drop into arrears if they couldn't pay one week. He trusted them to bring it up to date. I wondered if when the union picked up the box and found the money was short they'd have thought my dad had been on the fiddle.

'What made this seem likely was that Dad's best friend was the assistant treasurer. He'd always been round our house – he was just like an uncle to us. But after my dad died he dropped us completely. He didn't even go to the funeral. Perhaps he thought my father had been dishonest.

'I can't say for certain but I feel that this message about the tin box was my father trying to get through to explain why the accounts didn't add up.'

Unfortunately for Les' father, a message from a medium is not likely to cut much ice with union officials – unless a steward from a south London suburb is reading this and says 'So the old boy was honest after all.'

William was in his sixties and living in Winchester when his wife passed away suddenly. His pride and joy were the model ships and trains he made which his wife dutifully displayed and dusted. But though he was good with paint and glue, William left the domestic finances to his wife and without her he found himself confronted with a whole pile of unpaid bills and no idea where the money might be to settle them.

A week after her death, William's wife came to him in a dream and said: 'The money is behind the Flying Scotsman.'

Next morning William looked behind his favourite model train on the sideboard but found nothing and thought his dream must have been purely wishful thinking. Yet it was so vivid he could not forget it and felt compelled to check again. He then saw that an envelope was tucked into a groove at the back of the train's display stand. It contained the money for the bills.

Very occasionally the person who has died can't make amends if the omission is a practical one. Kirstie, who lives on the Isle of Wight, told me the following story.

'We were caring for my husband's widowed aunt after she became ill. For many years my aunt's sister-in-law took care of her, until finally she grew too infirm. We then took over. One morning when I was due to go round to fix her lunch my husband Reg said, "You stay in bed, I'll get a nice bit of fish for Aunty's dinner and pop in and cook it for her in my break."

'I fell asleep again but when I sat up, feeling much better, I saw an old lady's face coming towards me. "It's Aunty," I said and as I spoke I could see two tears like pearls running down her cheeks. Then the face faded and the moment was gone.

'In the middle of the morning Reg popped in. "Aunty's dead. I found her sitting in the armchair." We found out later she'd died at about the time I'd seen her face.

'No wonder she'd been crying: she never had got round to writing out her Will. All the money went to her brother, who drank it all away in a very short time. His wife, who'd done so much for Aunty, saw not a penny.'

James, who lives in Birmingham, telephoned me because of strange happenings in his house. Big stuffed toys and ornaments were moving to different positions, a missing earring disappeared and then appeared in the same place a week later and – the latest in the series – a gold bracelet that was tugged from his girlfriend Diane's wrist in the night then vanished.

It sounds like the classic case of a haunted house. But the incidents had started in James' *previous* house, when keys went missing and objects were moved.

A case of a poltergeist? Yet the presence seemed friendly and indeed had apparently saved Diane's life the previous week. She had been standing on the kerb waiting to cross the road when she felt a hand on her shoulder pulling her back. Seconds later a car hurtled round a corner at top speed. It would have knocked her down if she had not been pulled out of the way.

An incident for the psychic investigator? No, because James himself had the answer. It was just a question of fitting the jigsaw pieces together. And indeed, many so-called hauntings have explanations much closer to home. In James' case the incidents hadn't started out of the blue.

'When did these things start?' I asked.

'The evening my mother died. I had gone to the cash machine

and it swallowed my card. I went into the building society to complain but when the cashier opened the machine, the card wasn't there.

'As I went out I felt in my pocket and the card was there all the time. When I got home I found out my mother had died.

'Mum had always said, "When I die if I can possibly communicate in any way I will." Mum herself had seen her dad sitting on her bed after his death. Then one day I remember she was dishing dinner when she suddenly dropped a plate. "My brother's dead," she said, though he had always been as fit as a fiddle. But at that moment miles away he was killed.'

So now James and I had a possible candidate for the presence. Was the spirit of his mother still around him? And most importantly, why? It didn't sound like an 'I love you' visit since clearly she was wandering around moving things. A persistent presence can suggest that the spirit is unhappy. I asked (as tactfully as I could) if there was any family conflict. Mums, dead or alive, can act as peacemakers.

'It's funny you should ask, because my dad turned completely against me after Mum's death and I was so upset I just stayed in my flat not eating or doing anything. It was then my keys and my lighter apparently disappeared and appeared in the same spot days later, though in that case as every other I turned the house upside down looking for them.

'If it is Mum,' he said, 'why should she seem to attach herself to Diane?' I asked him if there were any other incidents apart from the car escape that involved his girlfriend.

'Yes, only a couple of days ago Diane felt someone touch her sleeve. And not long after Mum died, Diane, who sells double glazing, knocked on a customer's door. The woman opened the door and asked her in and said, "Who's this you've brought with you?" because she was only expecting Diane. "No one," Diane replied, and when she stepped inside the woman said, "Sorry, I was sure there was someone behind you." '

I told James of the many cases I'd discovered where the grief is so great that a relative will return to a close friend or a partner of the person left behind, just as in life we sometimes talk to our children's partners about issues that may be painful to the children themselves. I told him the story of Marnie, from British Columbia in Canada, whose mother appeared not to Marnie herself but to her friend Vickie.

They were sitting around the coffee table at work when Vickie said to Marnie, 'Your mother visited me last night, Marnie. She was just an outline at the window. She was holding a little red light in her hands.'

Vickie said this in a very matter-of-fact tone and Marnie took it very matter-of-factly, too. She said, 'Oh yes, she visited my friend Flo once in a dream. My mother kept saying, "Tell Marnie it's all right; tell Marnie it's all right." Then Flo woke up and could still hear Mum saying, "Tell Marnie it's all right." Flo was very upset because she didn't know what was supposed to be all right. But I knew. The afterlife, of course.'

At this point Vickie interrupted to ask, 'Why didn't she come directly to you, then?'

Linda, another friend, said she believed probably a wall of emotion was blocking direct contact and so it was easier for Marnie's mum to talk through a family friend.

This story seemed to make sense to James and we promised to keep in touch.

Two weeks later I heard from James again. 'Diane's toys are still moving and being stood on their heads. Her bracelet hasn't come back yet. Mum seems the most likely explanation and we've said hello, etc., but some things don't fit.'

'Like what?' I asked.

'Why should she take jewellery?' James asked.

'You tell me. Was there any trouble over jewellery after her death?

'Well, I know Mum once took a fancy to some earrings I owned and was going to sell. She went on about these earrings so much I said "OK mum, why don't you borrow them for a while. But I must have them back." Then when she died my dad gave them to my sister. It has caused quite a rift because he has given other jewellery I lent her to my sister, including a bracelet.'

So maybe mum was trying to tell James it wasn't what she wanted. We don't know what kind of communication is possible from beyond. If you wanted desperately to tell someone you hadn't intended the earrings to be given away, maybe grabbing an earring is one way of trying to express your frustration. The more I heard the more it seemed to me that poor old mum was unlikely to be at rest.

'Was everything as she would have wanted in her funeral arrangements and after her death?'

'It certainly wasn't,' said James, 'and I feel I was badly treated. Large sums of money I lent my family to buy their house have not been repaid. Also, Mum wanted her ashes buried with her mum and dad and brother and daughter, but my father didn't do that. I was very upset and told him so.'

So James was upset and maybe mum could see that he was upset and that the only person helping him was Diane. Unfinished business seems a powerful inducement for the dead to hover around.

The bracelet hasn't returned. Maybe it won't till the earthly issues are sorted and James is happy. Maybe that's what mum's trying to say. Perhaps when mum sees James and Diane have put the injustices behind them, things will no longer move except when mum pops back for a tidy. After all, old habits may never die.

Perhaps the underlying message of all these experiences is that we have to resolve matters ourselves so that the ghosts can rest. Maybe Les should confront the union officials and Richard should try a bit of earthly intervention about the Will.

Some people prefer not to think about their own funerals and believe such details are unimportant. Others want this final earthly act to be as organized as possible. Few of us, however, would be as dogmatic as Marlene in ensuring her send-off was correct down to the last piece of madeira cake.

Marlene was the matriarch of the family and as she lay dying she sent for her younger sister, Violet. No words of love or reconciliation were to pass her lips, however.

'People will have come a long way for my funeral. Make sure there are plenty of cucumber sandwiches and Earl Grey tea. I shall be in the next room so I shall know if you have got it wrong.'

All was duly prepared. It wouldn't have been surprising if Violet had conjured up the spectre of her disapproving older sister. But it wasn't Violet who saw Marlene, nor even her younger brother Ronald, equally under Marlene's rod of iron. Ronald's wife was standing in the drawing room at tea-time when she saw Marlene and her dead mother viewing the proceedings with gimlet glance.

'It wasn't till afterwards,' Ronald's wife told me, 'that I realized I hadn't seen them in the ordinary way because they were behind me and I hadn't turned round.'

Funerals are sad affairs in Britain – on the whole we have lost the ability to celebrate someone's passing. Yet recalling the old jokes and family stories at such a time can enable us to remember the person as he or she really was, with faults and prejudices as well as virtues. If we feel obliged to sentimentalize or put on pedestals those with whom we laughed and sometimes disagreed in life then we are alienating ourselves from the real person we knew. For Felicity, a reminder of her real 'grass-roots' dad came at his funeral. Felicity told me that her dad was very anti-church and found living in a former vicarage hard enough. When he died and mum fixed up a full Christian burial service he felt obliged to register a protest.

'The bearers were carrying the coffin when suddenly for no apparent reason it tipped sharply and almost toppled them over. Then when we went back home after the service all the doors were locked and not one of the family could find a key to get in. They'd all just disappeared. You can imagine the chaos, and an evening of flying books and crashing ornaments convinced us Dad was not amused.

'But Mum took it all in her stride.

'"That's just your dad paying us back for burying him in the church," she said with a laugh.'

Though it may be possible to express regrets for business not finished from beyond, it is better to leave our earthly affairs in order while we can. While I'm not suggesting you live every day as your last, it's no bad thing to have your house in order and not at all morbid to make sure that your partner and children know exactly what provisions you have made for them. There is nothing more bitter than a family squabbling over 'what Mum would have wanted' at a time when they should be united in grief and fond memories. And again, the time is now to tell your family you love them, forever.

9

Reconciliation in the Afterlife

We know our parents and older relatives will one day die and we hope that despite any irritations or bad feeling between us our love will be expressed before their passing. However in some cases the words of love remain unspoken and there can be great regret as well as grief to cope when a parent dies and bad feelings remain unresolved.

In the last chapter I talked of unfinished business in the practical sphere. Yet it is the angry words spoken or the love unspoken that can do the greatest damage to those left grieving. Many adults walk about bearing the scars or carrying a burden of guilt over not having reached an understanding with a dead parent. 'Too late' are sad words indeed.

But it is not always too late. The ties that bind can go on and bring reconciliation from beyond the grave. For me this is the most exciting aspect of the experiences I uncovered. It forms a basis for psychic family therapy – if psychologists and counsellors are willing to accept psychic experiences as they would any other insights offered by clients.

Many mothers say they would lay down their lives for their children. Thankfully, few are called to do so.

Gertrude lived with her mother on the eastern borders of Germany during the Second World War. With the prospect of an Allied victory came the news that the Russians were advancing, bringing with them an occupation just as ruthless to the people of the area. There was a car leaving the village for the west, with one seat vacant. Gertrude did not want to leave her mother behind to an uncertain fate, but the old lady insisted: 'I am old and I have lived my life. Now it is your turn. Go with my blessing.'

Gertrude did reach freedom but at first could get no news of her mother. Eventually she heard her mother had died. She always felt great guilt that she had left her mother behind, a guilt that remained as she built a successful life for herself. Many years later, Gertrude's mother came to her in a dream and embraced her and said: 'It's all right.'

Though the words were simple they were the blessing Gertrude needed. She no longer felt guilty because she knew that her mother had wanted her to go and approved of what she had made of her opportunities.

How much faith can we put in a reconciliation that takes the form of a dream? Again I would argue that the proof of an experience is not as important as the comfort it brings. Those who have had such dreams argue that they are different in quality and intensity from even the most vivid dream or nightmare.

Ruby lost touch with her in-laws after acrimonious divorce proceedings from their son, although he had in fact been unfaithful for years. Ten years later Ruby heard quite by chance that her ex-father-in-law was dying in hospital.

'It was strange,' Ruby said 'because although we lived in different parts of the country I'd had two very strong dreams over the previous week of going to see Wilf and his wife though there had been no special reason to think of them. In fact things were going so well in my life that I scarcely gave my old life a thought. My ex-husband, whom I saw occasionally when he took the children on holidays, maintained the fiction that the old man was well, though I later found out he'd been seriously ill for some time. In the dreams Wilf asked if I would go back to his son. I refused and explained I was happy in my new life and Wilf said he was glad and regretted the misunderstandings between us and would like to keep in contact. This was most unusual since he was a somewhat sour old man. In fact the only occasion I can remember him chuckling like a child was when he heard the novelty record "Mouldy Old Dough", a hit in the mid-seventies. He would march on the spot to the record, stamping his feet and whistling.

'It was a Wednesday morning when I heard that Wilf was dying. Ironically I had to break the news to his son, for he was due at my house to collect the children for a day out and his mother had phoned me. All day I could feel Wilf fighting and struggling against dying – he was always stubborn and a great fighter. By the evening I could see him lying in the darkened ward and I said "Let go, Wilf, accept it," and I felt him ease.

'It wasn't till later I heard he'd finally died early on the Thursday morning, alone as his wife and son had left the ward for a rest. Early Thursday morning I was sitting having a cup of coffee before the children woke. I suddenly saw Wilf standing in the middle of the room, whistling and marching on the spot to "Mouldy Old Dough". It seemed totally ludicrous. Then someone called his name, a woman's voice. He turned and pointed to himself, "Me?" He was like a schoolboy being unexpectedly picked for the school football team. I'd seen him feign surprise when given an unexpected compliment, but here he looked like a beaming child. Then he was gone.'

Ruby draws no conclusions from the story, other than that Wilf perhaps recalled a happy moment in his life with her and, in the absence of his wife and son, had on the point of death, wanted to be with the only other person to whom he had once been close.

An unhappy marriage can lock even adult children in a dependency trap. In 1967 Lindsey was 18 and set to leave her Midland home to go to college in Oxford. Her mother said she would die if left alone with her husband. Lindsey went amid many tears and resentment. Her mother refused any contact.

Halfway through the first term came an urgent message that Lindsey's mother was very ill. Lindsey rushed to the hospital to be told her mother was terminally ill and nothing could be done. She gave up her college place to nurse her mother at home through the last weeks but her mother died, blaming Lindsey for causing her illness. Now, some 25 years later, Lindsey continues the story:

'I realized on a logical level that there was no way I was to blame for my mother's death, but I found I was always trying to make amends. Eventually I had therapy and talked my guilt through and that was the end as far as I was concerned. But last week I had a dream in which I was going to Edinburgh University. Mum was chatting happily when she suddenly said: "Will you be coming home next weekend?"

'I replied it was too far and to my amazement she said: "Don't worry. I'll be fine without you."

'So Mum let me leave home 25 years on. Call it post-psychology projection or whatever but for the first time I feel free.'

I have been told many mother/daughter guilt experiences. The conflicts seem to come to a head when the mother is ill and the daughter must care for her. For many women the mother/daughter bond is still being worked out years after mum's death.

Julia, who lives in Berkshire, had a good relationship with her mother but still felt very guilty about her death because her mother had complained that the doctor hadn't cared for her properly during her last illness. Julia had always felt perhaps she could have done something more at the time. Though guilt after someone's death is a recognized part of the grieving process, only the reassurance of the dead person can sometimes dispel unjust accusations fully. Yet Julia finally went to a medium for a completely different reason.

'I went to the medium because it was six years after Mum died and I wanted to know if she could see my children who had been born since then. I wanted to contact her and I wanted to know if it was true that life went on. I missed my mum desperately when my children were born. She had seen my sister's children before she died.

'My sister and I decided to go to London for the day because we had been born there. I suppose we wanted to see the old places together and feel close to Mum.

'We went to look at two houses the family had lived in, to see my sister's old school and to trace the route by which Mum would have pushed me home in the pram. On the way back we came upon this lovely old building, The Spiritualist Association of Great Britain, so we went in. It seemed the right thing to do.

'There was a medium there and straight away she said she'd got our Mum. The medium told us what we'd been doing that afternoon, that we'd been to see our old houses and my sister's school. She even told us how Mum had died. It was wonderful to think while we'd been thinking about Mum all afternoon and feeling so close to her that she'd been with us.

'The medium said that Mum said I mustn't feel guilty about not complaining about the doctor. I can't tell you what a weight it was off my mind. The medium also said: "Your mum says the more you work, the more you will enjoy it and you mustn't feel guilty about it because if you're happy then you will make everyone else happy."

'Work was very much on my mind. I had started working weekends when my younger child Lawrence was seven months old to ease things at home financially. But I had felt very torn, especially as I was enjoying getting out of the house and meeting people at work. "Tell your dad about me," Mum insisted.

'Dad had always kept quiet about the psychic so I had no idea how he would feel if I told him that we had been to see a medium. But I did tell him six months later. He had been devastated by Mum's death. To my surprise he wasn't shocked. Now whenever he sees me he asks me, "Have you seen Mum? Has she come through?"

'It has opened up a whole new line of communication for us and made it easier for us to talk about Mum. And when I am feeling down or have a problem, suddenly the radio or the taps will turn on even when I am alone in the house and I am convinced it is Mum's way of letting me know she is still there for me. This direct contact began about a year after my daughter Laura was born. I know she is there and I wouldn't want to see her but it's nice that when I'm in trouble I talk to her in my mind and feel better the next morning.'

Julia's latest contact with her mother answered her original question, 'Does my mother know about the children?'

'I went for a psychic weekend in Abergavenny and a medium was giving a demonstration. It was 9.50 at night and the session was meant to have finished at 9.30. All night I'd been asking Mum in my head to come through because I had a lot of little things on my mind. The medium said, "I can't finish because there's a very persistent lady here who's been on my back all night and says her daughter's yelling out for her." She came to me. "Your mum says she's got her arms round you and is giving you a big cuddle."

'Though it was 14 years since her death, there were tears pouring down my cheeks because sometimes I still miss her so much. Then the medium said: "Your mum says she was at your daughter's party recently and there's another party coming up and you'll smell her perfume and know she's there."

'The second celebration was my niece's eighteenth birthday party. During the morning of the party my sister, who has never sensed Mum before, kept smelling her Blue Grass perfume.'

Julia's experiences with her mother have been entirely positive and a medium provided a good way of beginning the contact that made Julia realize her mum was still around.

Even where there is no guilt, the trial of nursing a terminally ill parent or relative may take such a toll that when the parent dies there seems nothing left and no point in going on. Carol nursed her father with cancer and when he died she could get no comfort from her husband or child, whom she had hardly seen during her father's illness. She believes that her father came back to help her to come to terms with his death by encouraging her each day to move a little way on her own as he had done when she was a little girl to make her go through the school gate without him.

'My dad became very ill with cancer. I helped to nurse him for 10 months and so I was totally devastated by his death though it was expected. Four days after he died I saw him at the end of the garden. I saw him there for several days before I finally went down the garden to ask him why he wouldn't come into the house. "Because it would make you cry," he replied.

'I can still years later hear him talking to me in my head as though he is here with me in the room and it is very comforting. But when he first died I needed to see him and hear him and have him close. I saw him every day and talked to him and it helped me gradually to adjust to life without his physical presence.

' "How are things, Dad?" I used to say and then I would ask him what I should do just as I used to when he was still alive. He always told me what he thought even if I wouldn't like it when he was alive and his advice was still the same.

'Gradually his image got fainter and fainter and he started to come less often. After a few weeks he was almost gone and I was dreadfully upset. He wasn't a particularly poetic man, but he told me the last time I saw him, "I will never leave you. I am here as long as you remember me, though you won't see me any more. I am in every flower you see."

'I find myself talking to Dad inside now and I see a column of blue light and I know he is there but it is so frustrating because I want to see him with my eyes. He says he's moved on and it can't be the same as when he was alive. I know he's right and I value his love which I know is with me, but I miss his physical presence.'

It is not always the big sins or misunderstandings that we regret after a person's death but the small omissions, the times when we were impatient or gave help grudgingly. Of course once the person has gone it is easy to forget the strains that we were under. And the one angry exchange can blind us to the day-to-day caring that we did provide.

Margaret, who lives in Cork, recalls:

'My father-in-law, who lived with my husband and myself, died suddenly. A few nights later I was in the kitchen drinking a cup of tea at about 11 p.m. I started to think about him. I had no regrets except for one incident. The week before he died his box of matches fell on the floor, scattering everywhere. I was cutting bread at the time and I thought, "Wait until I'm ready to pick them up."

'By the time I went to do it, he had struggled to pick up every one of those matches himself, which must have cost him so much effort. I was so sorry because I could have left what I was doing.

'I remembered the incident as I sat alone in the kitchen and I said a silent prayer, "Grandad, wherever you are, I hope you can hear me – I'm sorry I left you to pick up those matches."

'Suddenly the window I was sitting opposite in the kitchen started to rattle loudly as if someone were trying to open it. I jumped up to phone my husband at work but as I went to lift the receiver I noticed the rattling had become very gentle and I realized no one was breaking in. Then it stopped. As far as I was concerned Grandad had heard my prayer and I felt so happy. I tried to shake the window next day but it wouldn't even move. My father-in-law was 82 when he died.'

These 'small' incidents are more important than earth-shattering premonitions or dramatic ectoplasmic manifestations because they demonstrate the love that must be the guiding principle behind any after-death experience.

When a parent dislikes a son or daughter's choice of partner then there can be a rift in the family. In the following two cases it is the dead person who acts as mediator, bringing about reconciliation between those left behind.

Grace's father came back after his death to put right the bad feelings and indeed to intercede on his son-in-law's behalf.

Grace remembers: 'I had been ill with pneumonia and we had no money and a small child to bring up. My husband was an artist and had exhibited pictures at the Royal Academy. I had married against everyone's wishes and no one had liked him, least of all my late father. An uncle gave me enough money to go and stay in a hotel in Brighton with my mother and my child. I had almost decided to leave my husband for good. We arrived at the small hotel at tea-time and about half-way through tea a lady and gentleman came in. I didn't take much notice of them but in the evening my mother and I were in the lounge and the lady was sitting alone at the other end of the room. Eventually she got up and said goodnight and my mother, who was very friendly said, "Going so soon?"

'But the woman turned to me and said she had been wanting

to speak to me because when she came into tea a man (who fitted the exact description of my dead father) had been standing beside my mother pointing to me. When she spoke to him later he had asked her to tell me that he took back all he had ever said about my husband and that I was on no account to leave him but I was to try and help him all I could. The woman was mystified by the whole business but her advice turned out to be good.'

If it is the married child that dies, then the unspoken resentment can easily be fuelled by funeral and financial arrangements and the small yet very important issues such as who keeps her trinkets and mementos. I met Gay at a psychic fair in Birmingham and she told me of her 36-year-old married daughter who had died from a long and painful illness only months after the wedding.

'I had to find out where Sarah was. The week she was buried I went to a medium who didn't know me from Adam. I didn't even tell her why I had come. I was scarcely sitting down when she said "Your daughter wants to thank you for the lovely flowers. You know they were her favourite roses and they were special to her."

'I had told no one I had ordered a bouquet that was identical to her wedding roses because Sarah had loved those flowers so much.

' "She says you're to stop crying inside", the medium told me.

'I had been putting on a brave front but hadn't fooled Sarah. It was so comforting to know she wasn't just gone after all that suffering. "Did you not see the sun shining on the coffin?" the medium said. It might seem to anyone who wasn't there a trite thing to say, but the funeral had taken place on a dull, miserable day and just for a second as if by magic the sun had shone and reflected on the coffin. At the time I had thought it was really beautiful. Now I know it had meaning.

'Then about three weeks after Sarah died, I was in the bedroom hoovering. Suddenly Sarah was there with me. She looked so well. "Oh hello, love," I said and then I remembered and my daughter was gone.

'I fell out with my son-in-law after the funeral. One day I was upstairs and I found a photo of him and Sarah. She looked so beautiful that I couldn't bear to throw it away so I decided to blank him out. "He was good to me, Mum," Sarah's voice said as clear as day and so I left the picture as it was.

'Another day I was just walking down the lane where my dad used to live, thinking of happier times, and again Sarah was there with me. She'd had her hair cut for the wedding but now her hair had grown very long. She looked so well and happy it lifted my spirits just to see her. She had been so ill and reduced to a shadow of herself. I can hardly bear to talk about it.

' "Are you all right, are you all right?" I asked her. But she just smiled and then she was gone.

'I had bought her a little ring years back and she had always worn it, even after she was married. Her husband had sold most of her things after she had died. I didn't care about anything else but that ring meant so much . . . but I was too proud to ask him for it.

'I went to another medium because I couldn't stop thinking about the ring. She told me I was upset about a ring but my daughter said I was to send loving thoughts to her husband.

'It wasn't exactly the message I wanted because my son-in-law and I hadn't spoken a word for almost a year. I really did try that night because, as Sarah had told me, he had made her very happy. And very shortly afterwards he sent back the ring and some of her other things to me. I've worn the ring ever since and I feel very close to her.'

In a few cases it is the spirit who cannot rest.

Peggy's mother turned after death from the unkind parent and uncaring grandma to the kind of guardian granny we met before in this book. The old woman returned to offer support not to Peggy herself, whom she bitterly wronged, but to Peggy's youngest daughter who was nicknamed Mink by the family.

Peggy, an antiques dealer who lives near Marlborough has a very close and caring relationship with her own children and grandchildren. She told me: 'My mother was infuriated when she discovered she was pregnant because it meant she had to give up a career. A son she might have accepted, but when she learned she had produced a "bloody girl" she turned her face to the wall and refused even to look at me. When I was 11 I had a nervous breakdown because of her cruel treatment and I was taken from her. She did not like my children and with all the continuing heartache she caused me and them throughout the years it is not surprising few tears were shed at her passing.

'Then one Christmas Eve my youngest daughter Mink, who was 19 and working in Sydney, Australia, and who couldn't get home for Christmas, rang me in a great panic.

' "Grandma's here. I got home and she was standing on the stairs." My daughter had taken one look at grandma and fled to phone me. I was at a total loss as to what the old lady wanted, so I phoned a friend, Catherine, who is a healer.

' "Don't you see?" Catherine told me. "The old lady wants to make amends and her youngest granddaughter is away from her family at Christmas so she has gone to be with her."

'She suggested Mink should go back in and say, "We are all prepared to forgive you if that is what you want. Thank you for coming to look after me at Christmas."

'Mink had taken refuge in the local pub at the bottom of the road so I phoned her there and told her to take her courage in both hands and go back to the house.

'The old lady wasn't there when Mink opened the door but Mink spoke to her all the same and was no longer afraid. As Mink drew the curtains when she went to bed she is convinced she saw my mother outside. My mother appeared twice over the Christmas period to Mink.

'Since that Christmas the old lady has always appeared when Mink is in trouble or in a difficult situation and everything always turns out well. She was there at the birth of Mink's first child. She never said anything – she never does – but just stood at the bottom of the bed watching and it was very reassuring for Mink.

'Her most recent appearance was when my son was due to have a serious spinal operation. Wherever we were in the world we all agreed to pray for and think of my son at the time of his operation. I sat concentrating. Then after two and a half hours Mink rang very excited to say, "It's all right, he'll be fine. Grandma's just appeared outside the window."

'Four hours later a phone call came to say my son was conscious and could move his toes. The operation was a success.'

What then can we conclude? That it never is too late to express regret and grant forgiveness.

Not all regrets involve misunderstandings or harsh words. Janine, who lives in Michigan, USA, was very close to her aunt.

> 'After a healthy life my dear aunt suffered a stroke at age 87. She couldn't speak but kept trying to tell me something as she lay dying. About 12 years later early one summer morning I woke up to the sound of very heavy footsteps coming up the stairs. I was frightened and thought I should get up quickly and be prepared because there was no one else home at the time. Then the noise stopped and there before me was a vision of my Aunt Ella. She simply said, "I love you, Janine," and I said, "I love you too, Aunt Ella." Just then I reached out to put my arms round her but nothing solid was there and the vision just disappeared. During all that time I found I couldn't get up because I felt paralysed. I have never been able to forget this incident because it was so dear to my heart. And it was not a dream, neither did it seem to be full reality.'

You may choose conventional means of counselling to reconcile you to any guilt or regret you may feel towards the person who has died (see the Useful Addresses chapter). Or you may find these issues resolved in dreams. Or you may want to devise a simple ceremony – perhaps dropping flowers in a river or penning a letter of love and then offering it to a candle flame – or if you are religious a simple private ceremony of some kind. But, as with all unfinished business, the best time for reconciliation is while all the parties are still alive.

It's not only parents and grannies who return seeking reconciliation. In every marriage there are ups and downs and if one of the partners dies suddenly during a down then there can be deep unspoken regrets. Molly is a medium in her sixties and the following story shows just what a jigsaw puzzle the paranormal is. We are given the most tantalizing proofs, then, when we almost have a story fit for any scientific journal or front page of a newspaper, the line fades or the story is unfinished.

'I was ill in bed with flu,' Molly told me, 'when the phone rang. It was a man seeking help but as I was feeling so awful I said I'd contact him in a couple of days. But guilt got the better of me and I sat up in bed and dialled his number. I told him to call me back straight away and I'd try to help (phone bills have to be paid by earthly means and many sessions are long). But in the split second between putting down the phone and him ringing again I was aware of his wife with me. "Don't let him say anything," she said, "but tell him straight away I forgive him for what happened and I send him all my love always. Tell him he keeps my pink scarf under his pillow and then he'll know it is me. Tell him I forgive him."

'The phone rang and I told the startled man he wasn't to say anything but that his wife forgave him and that she had told me about the pink scarf.

'He was almost crying with relief. "Thank you, thank you," he said, "at last I can sleep again at night." '

'And?' I asked Molly.

'And what?' she replied.

'What did he do that she had to forgive him for?'

'That's not for me to ask or know,' she said 'though I could hazard a pretty good guess, as can most wives.'

10

Undying Hatred

Spirits may return seeking reconciliation but they may not always find a welcome here on earth. And where a vendetta in life has been particularly bitter it can continue even in death.

It was a difficult evening for Shirley, a medium who lived in Croydon. She was doing her best at a spiritualist church but was being rebuffed in no uncertain manner. 'I came to an old chap I'd never seen at the church before,' she told me. 'I picked up the presence of a woman who passed away several years ago and I described her down to the last button to him because I had such a clear picture of her. "No," replied the man, "nothing to do with me."

'But the connection was so strong I persisted. Still he denied all. Then a much younger woman called Mary who had died recently came through and I tried again, describing her in great detail. "Oh, that's my wife," he said with great pleasure.

'I was asked to give the man a lift home as he didn't have any transport. "Are you sure you can't place the first woman I described to you?" I asked him as we drove along, more as a conversation filler than anything else.

' "Oh I know who she bloody well was all right," he said. "That was my first wife – she gave me 30 years of absolute hell. I wasn't going to give her the satisfaction of talking to her. Now *Mary* was my second wife and we never exchanged a cross word. I was really pleased when she turned up. But life wasn't a bed of roses with the first one, I can tell you." '

Reconciliation can take place at any time but in a minority of cases it seems at least one party is refusing to accept the olive branch. As in all matters calling for diplomacy there is no point forcing the issue. Perhaps the only thing to do is to persuade the earthly combatant that, however justified a cause, sometimes it is better to walk away.

I had this forcibly brought home to me while I was doing a phone-in programme on my local radio station on the Isle of Wight. One of the callers, Suzanne, related what seemed to me like an attempt at last-minute reconciliation. But Suzanne was having none of it.

'We had a big family argument several years ago and since then I've not seen my parents and my nan has refused to speak to me. One morning a few weeks ago I had the most terrible feeling come over me that something really bad had happened but it wasn't till the next day at about 11 a.m. that I discovered that my nan had died suddenly at the time I'd had the feeling.'

Suzanne was puzzled that she should have had this experience in view of the gulf between her and her grandmother. I suggested that maybe her nan had reached out with her dying thoughts to try to heal the breach.

'You don't know my nan,' she said. 'Time and time again we passed her at the end of the street and she wouldn't even acknowledge me. And she was always unpleasant even before the row. Can you imagine a woman who would buy other children an ice cream and leave her own grandchildren out? My nan did. She's never tried to put things right between us. The last quarrel was just the last straw.'

'Well maybe at the last, when your life is supposed to run before you, she did have regrets and wanted to be with you.'

Suzanne wasn't convinced, though she felt it was strange she should link in to her nan's death and that therefore the occurrence must be more than a coincidence and have some meaning. What is important is not what I or anyone else thinks about any of these experiences but what they mean to the people who have them. Even if Suzanne's nan was trying to put things right, it wasn't accepted as such. It would be nice, albeit unlikely, for Suzanne and her parents to be reconciled as a result. Families can be remarkably stubborn when they feel their principles are at stake. And maybe nan's thoughts of her granddaughter weren't positive even at the end. We can't know. But the dying link does mark the end of a phase, and Suzanne could perhaps bury her own resentments along with her nan and in her own family life make sure the older generation's mistakes would not be repeated.

It's not only parents with whom vendettas can continue beyond death. Rivalry between siblings is common in life and is often initiated and indeed fuelled by parents who consciously or unconsciously encourage their children to compete for their affection. It is a cruel power ploy and many lives have been blighted by the feelings of being second-best as a child. Margot was the eldest of two children and was born during the Second World War while her father was away fighting. As in many cases, when he returned Margot could not accept him because he was a total stranger who had come suddenly into her life.

When Margot was two her sister Linda was born. Her father idolized the new baby from the first day. When Linda was four her appendix ruptured and she died. Margot always had the feeling, perhaps unjustly, that her parents wished she had died instead and even as an adult she felt she was second in her parents' affections compared with her dead sister.

When Margot was in her late twenties she visited a clairvoyant who told her that her sister Linda wanted to talk to her. Margot was very upset by this. Linda said it was their parents' fiftieth wedding anniversary and that she wanted Margot to buy some yellow rose bushes and say they were from Linda with love. Of course Margot couldn't admit to her father she'd been to a clairvoyant and that the rose bushes were from Linda as he was opposed to anything that smacked of the paranormal. But Margot bought the rose bushes anyway. Needless to say they were the favourite present. Linda had got it right again. What is more, on mum's birthday out came the very first golden rose.

Margot was deeply distressed by the experience, feeling that, even from above, Linda couldn't put a foot wrong. Many grieving parents do inadvertently make the surviving child feel unwanted. In my book *The Psychic Power of Children* one woman relates how when even in her mid-forties and a success she still felt she constantly had to live up to her golden-haired little sister who had died at the age of six. In life, favouritism towards one child can be outgrown or simply accepted as one of life's injustices. But the rival child who dies is frozen forever in perfection: the smiling golden-haired child in the picture frame whose sins are forgotten and whose virtues increase with the years.

But is it just the living who are guilty of playing favourites? I was having my long-suffering washing machine repaired when I heard the story of a grandmother who seemed to be just as bloody-minded in death as in life.

Over a cup of tea, the repairman told me about his girlfriend Tina's granny who had always disliked her eldest daughter Louise and continued the quarrel almost to her last breath. The old lady vowed she'd come back to haunt her daughter and never give her a minute's peace. For her part, Louise, tired of her mother's haranguing, said, 'I'll be glad when you are dead,' words many of us have spoken when provoked by difficult relatives.

As a result Louise was feeling pretty guilty as she prepared the funeral tea, wishing she'd humoured her mother more and thinking about the old girl's good points. As she formed the remorseful thoughts, glasses started flying off the sideboard. At every subsequent family gathering organized by Louise crockery would smash as though hurled by an invisible hand and things would inexplicably tip over.

Louise inherited her mother's house and what had been a quiet home (when mum wasn't reading the Riot Act) seemed to take on a life of its own. Doors banged and windows rattled even when there was no wind.

A case for the priest or a psychic investigator? No, a reminder that the dead don't become saints overnight. Maybe never. As the late

Stanley Plimsoll, a wise Quaker from Reading once pointed out, old age does not make a person more saintly or more unpleasant: a difficult old person may well have been a difficult young person and an obstreperous middle-aged person. Or, as the French singer Georges Brassens put it more acidly: 'Time has got nothing to do with the matter, when you're a b— , you're a b— .'

It would seem that death can have a false 'sanctifying effect' and much unnecessary anguish can be caused because we feel it is wrong to feel negatively towards people who while alive made our lives a misery up to the last and had no regrets whatsoever. It can be a tremendous relief to realize that mum may still be an old bag even at the pearly gates and is probably giving St Peter as hard a time as she gave us.

But the case of Louise and her mother was not a straightforward one. The effects were more far-reaching and potentially damaging, for Louise's mum continued to play off one family member against another, in death as she did in life.

Tina, whom my washing machine repairman brought to meet me, was only 13 when Louise's mother died. Tina used to sit with the old lady while she was ill. 'About two weeks after the funeral I was tidying my bedroom and I could suddenly smell Nan's scent. She used to get me to pick roses for her in the summer and she would make rosewater to dab on her wrists. The sudden smell of rosewater heralding Nan's presence went on for years. Once when I got in my boyfriend's car I told him, "Nan's here," because the perfume in the car was so strong. It was as if she had walked straight through me. We watched our step that evening, knowing Nan was watching.

'I was always very close to Nan as she had brought me up for much of the time. The last time I sensed her around me was when I was just 18. Nan had a beautiful 60-year-old ring she always said I would have on my eighteenth birthday. Just before she died she told my mum I was to have the ring when I was 18. Now I have it I hardly ever smell her perfume. It's as if now I have the ring I don't need to be reminded of her.'

A touching tale made more so by the fact that grandad still talks to his dead wife and she kisses him goodnight. Yet the same loving nan makes her eldest daughter's life hell. Indeed, her most recent dramatic appearance was at Tina's eighteenth birthday party organized by her aunty Louise, when inevitably the glasses went flying about.

In few cases is the favouritism (or its opposite) as blatant as this. But obviously if nan is shedding perfume and benign thoughts in one direction and flying glass in the other, then Louise and Tina are mourning two very different people. Psychologists would have a field day if Louise, Tina and nan could sit around the family therapy table.

This case certainly destroys the angel/demon divide, unless nan has a foot in both camps. Of course nan may not realize the havoc she is causing. She may just be sitting on her cloud, seething about her eldest daughter who, in her eyes, probably hasn't put a foot right since she crawled out of carrycot, while sending fond thoughts to her beloved granddaughter, who for no particular reason has always come up smelling roses where her nan is concerned.

If family feuds are forever, then when it comes to battles beyond the grave the same rules apply as on earth: if you are not family then stay away from them if you can. Interfering in your neighbours' affairs is risky at the best of times. It's even worse when you're dealing with a ghost.

Some ghosts may have suffered at the hands of their family and, in their need to tell their version of the truth, come back to a friend or even the inhabitants of their former house to complain of wrongs their family did perhaps many, many years before. At first the ghost may seem menacing but may well be angry not with the person he appears to but with someone who is also dead. Thus you can find yourself caught in the middle of someone else's family feud.

The story Andrea tells gives rise to the question: why didn't the ghost go to the person against whom her rage was directed?

For the offender lived only a few doors away. Andrea told me how she found herself confronted by one very angry spirit.

'There was a woman – it was like seeing her on a big television screen. She looked very severe with her hair rolled in a bun and fifties-style glasses. "I hate Dave, I hate Dave," she was screaming over and over again. Dave was the name of our neighbour, from whom we had bought our house.

'She was so angry it was terrifying, but it wasn't until later I discovered her identity. Another neighbour, an old lady who had lived in the street since she was a child, told me the woman had been Dave's father's wife.

'Dave's father (James) and his wife had never had any children. This had upset James so much he found himself a woman in Plymouth who bore him a son. When his wife died he moved his mistress and her son into his house. I found a picture of James' wife in the attic many years later when I was clearing it. It was taken on her wedding day but she was unmistakably the woman I had seen. I had never forgotten her or the fierce hatred she had for Dave. After all, Dave was the son of the mistress and had inherited the house that the wife regarded as hers.'

If you do know the people involved, as Andrea did, it can be very difficult to know whether to pass on the communication or to leave things lie. And what when the injured party lived hundreds of years ago but returns to disturb your peace of mind?

Beryl moved into in an Elizabethan house in the north country. Her 20-year-old daughter became the victim of the 'haunting'.

'A man in the dress of years ago appeared time and time again in most terrible dreams when my daughter slept in her room. It was as if the room changed as it would have been in another century, with a four-poster bed. The man would cry, "I didn't deserve to die." He told her that his son had killed him many, many years before but had made it look like an accident. He wasn't hostile to my daughter but it was very frightening for her. At last we called in the local priest who was very sympathetic and carried out a blessing ceremony in my daughter's room, where the man said he had been killed. The activity ceased. I hope the man found peace.'

I think that reliable outside intervention when other people's family ghosts are distressing you can be helpful. I think attempts at ghost-hunting or amateur seances are risky at best, if only in terms of the psychological problems they can cause. I wouldn't recommend you wade into other people's quarrels in life and would suggest professional intervention when you are dealing with an unknown element. Full-blown exorcisms with bell, book and candle are not undertaken lightly even by priests and the well-meaning amateur really is playing with fire. Modern blessing ceremonies, favoured by many priests and healers, can perhaps bring comfort to all involved, most of all to some poor ghost who doesn't want to be cast into outer darkness but desires peace wherever he may be.

Sometimes a spirit, though unrelated to your family, can mirror a personal crisis in your own life. It is here that the psychic, physical and psychological can make a pretty explosive cocktail. Pauline's story is interesting because she had to deal with enemies beyond and before the grave. An intelligent and sensitive woman now in her sixties living in the south of England, Pauline still has vivid memories of her father's second wife although she only met the woman once, when she was 11 and living in Tasmania. Her father had brought the woman to the house as his mistress and ordered Pauline's mother into the street.

Pauline remembers giving the woman a well-deserved kick in the shins. But her stepmother's challenge from beyond the grave gave Pauline the incentive to fight for survival many years later.

In 1979, when Pauline was in her early fifties and living in England, she was about to undergo a serious operation. The night before the operation she dreamed of her red-haired stepmother standing in front of a house in Australia telling her, 'You'll never set foot in my house.'

'Oh yes, I will,' Pauline insisted. And she told me: 'Then followed a battle of wills in which I mobilized my own strength for the operation if only to defy my stepmother and go to my father's house.'

When she recovered Pauline wrote quite spontaneously to the father she hadn't seen for 30 years, saying she forgave him. A letter returned from her dad telling her that his common-law wife, whom Pauline had seen in her dream, had died the previous year. He offered to pay her return air-fare if she would go out and stay with him in Australia. Not only did Pauline have the satisfaction of stepping inside the stepmother's house, she also helped her father's new wife take all the stepmother's belongings to the rubbish tip.

Pauline's father died recently, but she has not been haunted by him for their business was finished. He left her nothing in his Will but she has a greater legacy than money, the sense that she has assigned her past relationship to its proper place. She is now writing the story of her life.

If you can't settle things in life then the only answer is to bury them as deeply as you can afterwards. One long-suffering son and daughter-in-law I know put a very heavy piece of Yorkshire stone on his mother's grave after she died mid-rage. They then went and blew the inheritance she'd left on an expensive holiday cruise, toasting the old girl at every port. They said goodbye to her at the last port of call and when they reached England got on with their lives with no regrets.

We can't make anyone value us, whether parent, grandparent, child or love turned cold. What we can do is refuse to live by others' assessments of our worth whether they are living or dead. Many a successful person still feels like the stupid, clumsy child, rejected by critical parents, even though those parents are long since buried. For some people, conventional counselling is helpful; for others a personal ceremony of goodbye to the negative influences of the past may prove healing. Refuse to accept the judgement of those who seek to diminish you.

11

Phantoms Need Families

What of the spirits who have been rejected by their own families? In *The Psychic Power of Children* I recount the strange tale of a little boy who died in a fire. His ghost returned and, as his parents had moved, he went to 'stay' with the people over the road whose children he had played with in life. Since then I have come across other, similar cases.

For instance, the Reverend Tom Willis told me: 'Sometimes children's invisible friends can be pure fantasy but sometimes their mum will see something and ring up saying "My little boy's got a ghost." If there are any other phenomena such as cold rooms then it's probably more than a childish fancy. At a youth club, an 18-year-old girl told me how her brother when he was six or seven would come down every morning with crazy old-fashioned jokes or riddles.

' "Where do you get them from?" his mother asked.

' "Oh, from the old woman who comes and sits on my bed."

' "What old woman?"

' "The one who is in my bedroom every night."

'The family thought it was his imagination but one day his mother was passing his bedroom door and heard a one-sided conversations, complete with pauses while the other person answered. She opened the door and peeped round and there sitting on the bed was an old woman in a nightdress wearing a fancy wide-brimmed hat. The mother was struck dumb and went downstairs not knowing what to do.

'She decided to try to find out the history of the house. The previous occupant had been an old woman and she had died in what was now the little boy's bedroom, sitting in a chair. She had obviously been trying a particularly beautiful hat on when she passed away, because when she was found she was wearing the hat although still in her nightdress.'

It seems amazing that some relatives will cross the world to maintain contact while others prefer to 'adopt' the new owners of their house. Perhaps this is because their blood ties weren't as great as their love of their former home. Connie's resident ghost seems to have adopted her because he had no friends or family. Connie soon realized that the inhabitant of her old house didn't come to cause trouble but simply for the bit of kindness he never found in life.

'We moved into our present house in 1944. My husband Ned was in the Navy and I lived in the house with my young son Peter. One day not long after we moved in I heard the front door open and I could hear someone walking heavily upstairs as though he was dragging a foot with a heavy boot on. I wasn't frightened. When the presence got to the top of the stairs it seemed to go into the back bedroom, which served as our bathroom. I heard the same sound again and again and always the sound stopped when it reached the bathroom. I made enquiries in the street and the old woman two doors down told me that a man called Old Rob had lived in our house. He had a club foot and used to sleep in the back bedroom. The house had been empty for 18 months before we bought it.

'Of course I remembered Old Rob. He had been quite a character in our town when I was young, always going through rubbish bins and picking up litter and junk. He had a hard time in those days because people used to make fun of his foot. I'd always wondered if he had a home.

'The visits carried on for a long time but I didn't mention it to my husband. But once when Ned came home on leave I left him at home babysitting. "Funny house you've bought here," he told me when I got back. "I could hear someone dragging a heavy foot upstairs but when I looked there was no one."

'Our "lodger" went on to cause a bit of marital disharmony. One night Ned and I were sitting together in the living room when suddenly every note on the piano sounded – down the scale, up and down again. I sat on the edge of my chair but my husband was having none of it. He insisted there must be mice in the piano and stripped it right down. There was nothing inside. But of course he couldn't get the piano back together so we had to get rid of it and I wasn't at all happy about that.

'I got used to having Old Rob round the place but one afternoon I sensed him coming into the living room with me so I said to him "Look I'm very happy for you to be here but why don't you come to the spiritualist church with me? Maybe they could help?"

'Months later I was at the spiritualist church and a medium said there was an old man with a club foot coming up the aisle towards me. He just wanted to thank me for accepting him. After that I never heard him again going up the stairs.'

It's bad enough when one's own elderly relatives arrive for a week's holiday that stretches into a month and start moving things round and generally disrupting routine. When the elderly aunty isn't even yours, and what's more has passed on, then being taken over ceases to be a joke. For Mike and Claire, the old woman who had previously occupied their house carried on her routine as normal, moving the ornaments and waking up the budgie when they'd put the cover over its cage for the night.

Though they were a down-to-earth couple they found the woman's presence a bit spooky and at last sent for a medium. Once the medium had made contact with the old woman, whose name turned out to be Dolly and who was (as they had concluded) the former owner, she suggested very tactfully that the old woman might like to move on to be with her loved ones. Could Dolly see her loved ones waiting? Yes, Mum and Sis were waiting for her.

But Dolly wasn't budging. The house meant more to her than any dearly departed waiting for her and as far as she was concerned her domestic arrangements would continue into eternity.

Was there someone Dolly was particularly attached to in her new family? 'Oh yes,' came the answer.

'Well, Dolly could pop back from time to time and say hello and make sure everything was up to scratch domestically.'

At last it seemed Dolly was prepared to go on. But there was another hitch. She wanted to say goodbye.

Was it the young couple she couldn't bear to leave?

No, it was Joey the budgie, to whom the old woman had formed a close attachment and from whom she was reluctant to be parted. For Dolly had had a budgie of her own who had been her closest companion in her last lonely days when it seemed the world had left her alone.

At last Dolly had gone her way, the budgie stayed quietly under its cover at night and nothing was moved. A happy ending? In a strange way the house was missing something without her. She never came back.

Marcia, the medium involved in this case, believes that in some instances exorcism can make the situation worse. Some so-called malevolent poltergeists may simply be spirits trying to be understood. Remember Joe and the disappearing earrings? After all, many elderly people are set in their ways in life and may not want to leave the home they have loved straight after their death, especially if they lived there for many years. Perhaps we should rethink the universe in terms of relationships and see spirits as people who have lived and loved and may form strong attachments to places, people or animals.

If you find a benign phantom has adopted your family, then just accept the odd bang and thud. Dolly was a noisy ghost and a bit of a nuisance but the couple never doubted she was friendly. Children don't seem at all worried by these things and if your child's invisible friend or family ghost is causing no harm then you don't need to send for the priest or medium. But in the cases of Old Rob and Dolly the activity ceased once an explanation was given, and in both psychological and psychic terms that equals a satisfactory solution.

Liz was pregnant and living in a big old house in East London when she and some friends played with a Ouija board. A man called Bob came through who said he had lived in Bow and had drowned in the Thames in Victorian times. He told Liz she would give birth to a little girl.

'I got really scared because I could see this man in a top hat and black cloak standing in the corner. After that I was afraid to be alone in the house. To my relief I had a little boy but 18 months later I had a girl. When Lucy was two and a half we moved and she told me her friend Bob was coming with us. Apparently Bob went everywhere with her and would sit by her bed at night chatting. When she was a bit older I asked her what Bob was like and she said he had a tall black hat and a long cloak. My blood ran cold though she wasn't in the slightest upset by him. A few months later we moved to Basildon.

' "Bob says he's not coming," Lucy told me, "He hates Basildon." '

If you have got a nasty adopted family member – you'll soon sense malevolence, whatever the cause – it's as well to seek outside help. I'm not saying this is easy. While every diocese has someone appointed as an exorcist, the attitudes of parish priests do vary from those who are totally sympathetic to those considerably less so. Don't be afraid to ask round different churches for understanding guidance, to seek the help of your local spiritualist church or to ask a reliable association (see the Useful Addresses chapter of this book). You have every right to ask for help and there is nothing to be ashamed. If there are any strong family tensions try to sort them out, especially if children are involved, but don't automatically accept someone else's word that the problem is psychological if you sense it's not.

The problem may not be getting rid of the new family member so much as claiming your stake in him. A family ghost, especially the more up-market mediaeval type, can be a very desirable asset, especially when it comes to one-upmanship at dinner parties with the people down the road.

Ann-Marie recalls: 'There was a grey man we had often seen in the garden of our house. Though the house was in the middle of a Berkshire town it had been built in the fifteenth century and had been in my husband's family for generations. Several new houses had been built recently in what were the old grounds and we'd invited two of the new couples over to get to know them.

'The grey man always looked so dejected that one day my husband went out and said to him, "What's wrong, old man? Is there anything we can do to help?"

'That was obviously the wrong conversation opener because the old man disappeared for about six months.

'We were finishing dinner with the neighbours when suddenly Anne from the house next door looked down the garden and said: "Oh, look, there's our grey man." "No, he's not,' insisted my husband, "we had him first." '

If you want a 'designer ghost' to add to your guest list, try the small ads. The hire-a-spirit business could take off in a big way.

12

Coming for to Carry Me Home

If we are very fortunate we can share the last moments of those we love. However painful the death, it seems that for a few moments we can see through the eyes of the dying the dimension beyond. Many have said their whole lives were changed by such a moment as they take mothers, fathers, aunts and uncles to the brink of life.

The old spiritual 'Swing Low, Sweet Chariot' talks of 'a band of angels coming . . . for to carry me home.' The idea is perhaps one that appeals and yet sense tells us it is not possible. But we have left the realms of reason for a place where only hope can sustain us.

'When I was 17,' Margaret, from Cork, explains, 'my cousin and I came from visiting an aunt who was very ill with cancer and suffering great pain. We went to church to pray that God would take her.

'A few nights later as I was going upstairs to bed I suddenly heard a beautiful heavenly choir outside the house. I ran downstairs. I couldn't wait to unlock the door so I opened the window of the sitting room. I was stunned to find nobody outside yet I could still hear this beautiful choir of about 60 voices singing out. One voice would sing and then they would all join in. It was very clear and beautiful but with no words I could understand. My mother, who had gone to bed just ahead of me, started calling me because she wanted to know why I had dashed downstairs and opened the window. She should have heard the choir but I realized she didn't. The time was between 11 and 11.05 p.m. I decided not to tell my mother about what I had heard that night.

'The following morning when my mother came home from

mass she told me that Auntie had died. I asked her whether it had been the night before between 11 and 11.05 p.m. and she asked me how I could possibly have known. I still did not tell my mother about the choir.

'At dinner-time my mother said, "I met your Aunt Katherine and she said your cousin Marina heard a choir at the back of her house last night at the time Auntie died. But Auntie Katherine couldn't hear anything." So then I told my mother I had heard the heavenly choir as well. I also asked my mother whether Marina had told her mother that she had heard first one voice and then the others joining in. That was just how she had described it. When I met Marina that evening I told her I had heard the choir at the same time, though nobody else had.'

Aunties orchestrating heavenly choirs may be the extreme, but it is often as if the family connection enables living relatives to share a glimpse of another dimension and perhaps receive some assurance that death is not the end.

When Nicola's mother died she saw not a golden light but her mother's spirit in the form of white rays. 'I was 38 when my mother died,' she said. 'While the coffin stood in the church I definitely saw my mother's spirit rise and leave her body as a substance made up of white rays. They were the same size as her body though without form. The white rays drifted to the side of the coffin and then upwards till they were three or four feet over the coffin and then disappeared. No one else shared my experience.'

Most frequently the dying see their departed relatives waiting to greet them.

Marje's mother had been very ill for years with heart trouble and hadn't walked unaided for a long time. On the morning she died she was dozing when suddenly she sat up bright as a button and demanded: 'Where's my hat and coat?'

'In the hall,' Marje replied, amazed because her mother hadn't even been strong enough to sit up in the chair.

'Well hurry up, your dad doesn't like to be kept waiting,' she said sharply.

Marje decided to humour her mother but by the time she had unearthed the things from the back of the cupboard the old woman had passed away.

Philip, who lived in Northumberland, was in his eighties and had been ill with cancer for some time but remained cheerful and lucid to the end. During the last week of his life he began to smile and talk to his mother who had died 50 years before. He also told his daughter he was going home.

'You are home,' said Glenys, for she had moved back into her widowed father's house to nurse him in the last months.

As he took his last breaths he smiled beyond her and tried to hold out his arms.

'For a second he looked like a kid seeing Father Christmas,' Glenys said, 'and his last words were not my name, nor his late wife's but "Wait for me, Mum." Though it's years ago I often wonder if he did see his mother again.'

Are these physiological phenomena caused by the brain cells dying and the brain being starved of oxygen or a psychological protective mechanism? The answer is that, until we can recreate the experience of dying in the laboratory, we can only see the wonder on the faces of those aged or in agony who on the point of death are transformed. Sometimes it may be that those they love can share this experience.

Leonard of North London told me: 'My Aunt Eleanor experienced a tremendously bright light one night as she lay in the darkness. She had lost a young son some years before. In the light there was a picture of her son running towards her mother-in-law saying, "I'm so pleased to see you, Grandma," and the following day she heard that her mother-in-law had passed away not long after the experience.'

Sheena herself saw the relatives who had come to fetch her father, though the old man would not go until his affairs were sorted.

'The night my father died I saw my mother and my fiancé (who had died of TB when he was 27) on either side of the bed, waiting to help him over. Then I heard a voice say, "He'll die when the first bird sings."

'All this was on the Thursday though the doctor said he would not last the night.

'On Sunday morning one of my brothers saw a great white light around the bed. When the first bird sang on Monday morning my father finally slipped away.

'Though the deeds of the house were where my father had told me, there was no Will. My brothers and I spent the day looking for it and the whole time my father haunted us all in turn as we looked through the drawers of his desk and his private papers.

'We could feel him behind us as we searched saying: "What are you doing going through my private papers, why are you looking in there?" It was as if he were behind us the whole time. This went on for another two days, as long as his physical body was in the house, and only ended after the funeral when the solicitors had all the papers. We found the Will eventually, tied up with a lot of old gardening papers.'

Sometimes the appearance of a dead relative can be a warning not of our own passing but that they have come to fetch someone close to us.

The first time Judy saw her dead grandad her grandma was ill in hospital. 'Have you come for Gran?' Judy asked him.

'Not this time, love,' he told her. 'Your gran will be fine. You've got to stop worrying and get on with your life. But I promise I will come and tell you when I am going to fetch her.'

A few years later Judy told me she was sitting in her living room in a chair facing the door when she saw her grandad beckoning to her on the stairs.

'Oh hello, Grandad, what are you doing here?' Judy said – to the amazement of her husband who was sitting on the settee opposite her.

She ran upstairs after her grandfather.

Her younger son Ian came out of his room and walked straight through the old man.

'I've come to collect your gran,' Grandad said, 'I promised I'd tell you when the time came.'

Judy's grandma was in hospital recovering from an operation. Judy phoned her dad who said that when he had seen gran that evening she was a bit better. But shortly afterwards the news came that she was dead.

Though Cynthia wasn't ill, she was not surprised to see her dead son Frank appear as she was in her eighties and had come to terms with her own mortality. Frank appeared to her suddenly in the night.

'You've come for me,' Cynthia said.

'No,' her son told her, 'not you, but I've come for someone close to us both. I'm here because I didn't want it to be a big shock when you heard bad news in the morning.'

Then Frank disappeared.

The next morning when Cynthia was told that her great-grandson had been killed in a road accident, she coped far better than anyone expected.

Why hadn't Frank identified who was to die? Perhaps because then the old woman might have felt she had to tell the family, which would have been distressing for her. We can only guess.

Piers' father lived in the south of England and had never had a serious day's illness in his life. Suddenly he appeared to Piers, thousands of miles away on business, in the middle of the night.

'I've always wanted to travel to exotic places,' his dad said, 'so here I am.'

It was exactly his father's humour, Piers reflected. Not long after the vision a telephone call came to tell Piers that his father had died from a heart attack at his home some hours before. A simple if tantalizing psychic encounter? Yes, but Piers had never got on with his father and deeply regretted the coldness between them that had grown up over the years. That his father should cross half the world to come to him at the point of death helped Piers to feel that there had been a deep bond between them in spite of any lack of warmth.

Adrian was on holiday in France when he had a similar though less direct experience. About 7 o'clock one morning he had what he describes as a terrifying and vivid nightmare.

'I saw a disembodied face. It was like that of my young son who was back in England but it was older – middle aged. The face began to recede into the distance. In the dream I knew what was happening and I kept shouting: "Don't go – come back." Then the face smiled. It was a smile of such incredible kindness, then it disappeared. When I woke up I told my wife, "I've had a death dream." I don't usually remember dreams at all but I kept referring to this one all through the holiday. At first I wanted to phone home to England or anywhere to find out what was happening. When I got back I found out that my father had died at 7.30 on the morning I had the dream.'

Adrian, an only child, had not seen his father for two years. 'We always loved each other but for the past 20 years we hadn't got on that well.'

Adrian had spoken to his father on the phone just before he went on holiday but heard nothing to lead him to suspect that the old man was ill. He died of a sudden brain haemorrhage which took everyone totally by surprise. He was dead before anything could be done.

'I'm so incredibly grateful that he came to me before he died. I don't believe he came from the "beyond". I think this was part of his death experience.'

I have collected several of these father/son deathbed encounters. Generally they seem much more straightforward and final than encounters between mothers and daughters, who often seem to have so many more deep-seated emotions to work through.

No death can be more poignant than that of a mother leaving a young child, so what could be more natural than that a mother's last act on earth is to go to her child to show that the loving can and will go on.

When Meg, who lives in Northamptonshire, was nine her mother was very ill. One night Meg woke up to see her mother standing at the foot of her bed and reassuring her that everything was all right now and that she was better. In the morning a relative woke her up and said she had something to tell her about her mother. Meg replied she knew it was wonderful. Her mother was better and she had seen her during the night and had told her herself.

One of the strangest things I have discovered while writing this book is that the actual time span surrounding a person's death is very hazy. Someone can appear in 'ghostly' form miles away to a family member days or weeks before his or her actual death. There is usually a purpose for the visit – typically a need to say goodbye. Death may not be, therefore, a once-and-for-all moment of being here and then not here, but a slow merging of the dimensions in which – for want of a better phrase – the astral body is freed.

Cicely, who lives in Hampshire, told me the following story:

'My maternal grandmother was the twelfth child of 13. Her father was head gardener on a large estate in Suffolk. They were living in a Georgian house at the end of their village street. One night the children were sitting in the firelight in the living room when they heard the front door open and their mother come in. She threw open the living room door and called, "Come in, Annie."

'Annie was her sister, who also lived in the village. Their mother turned round but Annie had gone. "That's strange," she told the children, "I've just walked the length of the village street with Annie but now she's gone."

'Soon afterwards the news came that Annie had died suddenly.'

This 'astral travel' is of course only one possible explanation for Elaine's experience with her godmother shortly before the old woman died. And we don't know whether the old woman herself had any awareness of the experience or even had a dream of travelling to Elaine's side.

Elaine was at work when suddenly she had an overwhelming feeling she was in the presence of her godmother, whom she called

Aunt Sara. Elaine felt so strongly that Aunt Sara was there that she found herself saying: 'Hello, Aunty, what do you want?'

She felt that her godmother had come to say goodbye. The feeling faded but when Elaine got home she told her husband and decided to write to her godmother to see if everything was all right. But as always time went by and she didn't get round to it that week or the next. Two weeks later the news came that Aunt Sara had died in her sleep. Elaine says she didn't feel as unhappy as she might have done had she not had the opportunity to part in love.

It may also be that the time after the physical body has died may be a period of transition and at this time the newly dead may turn to the living for comfort. Dianne, who lives on the Isle of Wight, told me of the following incident which occurred when she was 18 and staying at her grandmother's home the night before her nan's funeral.

'It was an old house in the middle of fields and I woke between sleep and being fully awake hearing my nan calling out "Dobby, please help me Dobby. Dobby where are you? I need you" over and over again. It was unmistakably Nan.

'Dobby was her name for Donna, the daughter who had lived with her and took care of her and when Nan was alive. She would often call for Dobby to help her find something she needed. The strange thing was I was the only one to hear her call out though Aunt Donna and my mother were in the house. I had always been very close to my nan. I felt she had discovered she was dead and was looking for her body and called out as she had done many times to Dobby for help.'

Perhaps death in war is the strongest incentive for a person to travel and be with those he loves in his last moments. Such stories abound. Ellen from Surrey explained: 'In 1917 my two brothers were serving in France where they had been since November 1914. The elder of the two was two-and-a-half years older than me. For most of our lives we had been very close having many tastes in common and doing many things together.

'On 22nd November, 1917, I had been having supper with a woman friend and walked home in the London blackout. I arrived home feeling very depressed. I asked my sister if I might share her bedroom that night. She agreed and for some time we lay awake talking. Finally we both fell asleep.

'Some time later I awoke and sitting up shouted my brother's name twice. My sister asked me what was the matter and I replied, "It is strange – I thought that he was in the room." As I called out he seemed to fade into the wall.'

'About 10 days later we received the telegram telling us he had been killed in action on the 22nd.'

But even in these saddest of cases come tales of rich humour that reveal the family as it is, loving and very true to life. These stories that offer us smiles amid sorrow are for me the strongest indication of the survival of the whole person after death.

What if a spirit can't attract his loved one's attention in a dream? What if the intended recipient remains blissfully unaware of all attempts at contact?

Alec is now in his eighties but he remembers this incident as clearly as though it was yesterday.

'In 1916, when I was eight years old, I lived in Wiltshire. My favourite uncle Tom was in the Wiltshire Regiment and had been missing for six weeks. One night when I was in bed I heard someone call my name. I thought I must be dreaming because at the foot of my bed stood my favourite uncle in soldier's uniform. "Go and wake Grandad, Alec," he said, "and tell him I want to talk to him."

'It was hard to wake Grandad because he liked a drink, but at last I shook him awake and he came grumbling and saw Tom too. But he wasn't scared, he just said: "How are you, lad?"

'I think as Grandad had had a few he probably thought Tom had arrived back in the middle of the night from overseas and was having a chat with me in my room.

'Tom said to Grandad: "Tell mother I'm not coming home again. Break it to her gently. I've got to go now. But don't worry about me because I'm very happy."

'Grandad insisted in the morning it had just been a dream. But he told my grandmum anyway, and my uncle never did come back.'

The Near Death Experience (or NDE as it is known) is perhaps a 'dress rehearsal' of these final moments and it may be of human as well as scientific interest that departed relatives are frequently seen in this mid-dimension world. Could it be that the relative beyond does come to the aid of a family member who enters the other world temporarily, especially if there's still work to be done on earth?

Patsy of Berkshire describes her mother's experience the day Patsy's husband walked out on her after 25 years of marriage. 'On the day Gavin left, Mum, who lived with us and had been very close to Gavin, had a very bad stroke. The priest was called and when he went back to the twelve o'clock mass asked the congregation to pray for Mum as she was dying.

'She recovered and afterwards in hospital she told me she had gone to a place where the light was really pink and everything was so lovely. My dad, who had died years before, was there waiting for her. But Dad told her: "You can't come yet. Patsy needs you to help her in her trouble," so back Mum had to come.

'My own dad had left Mum for a time when I was young so he knew how hard it was for a woman alone. In a way letting Mum come back to me when I was in the same boat was a chance for him to make up for it a generation on. When she recovered Mum was a tower of strength to me and now she is old it is my turn to care for her. She often asks now to go home to her mother and before long I think she will.'

Julia told the story earlier in this book of how her mum had come back after her death through a medium to tell Julia she mustn't feel guilty for not making a fuss about the doctor's apparent neglect. But Julia's mother had already had a brush with death when Julia herself was born.

'Mum was desperately ill when she was giving birth to me as she had pneumonia and the strain was too much. She actually died for a moment. The surgeons resuscitated her but Mum remembers floating above the operating table and even following the doctors into the corridor to report (incorrectly) to Dad that I was a boy. She repeated word for word their conversations including the words spoken in the corridor. But then Mum went on to a place where she met her own dad, who had died not long before Mum was born. Mum had never ever seen a photo of her dad because there was a certain amount of mystery surrounding him. He and her mum had never married.

'Her mother always said he had died of a broken heart for his native Ireland but it may have been that in those days it was such a disgrace not to be married that Gran was romanticizing what had happened. When Mum recovered she described the man she had seen to Gran. Gran was very shocked because the description of her "husband" was so accurate. But Mum also said that she felt a presence leaving her as she came back to this world and she wondered whether she had left part of her spirit behind.'

When people see relatives they don't know in NDEs then it raises the question of whether the phenomena can possibly be dismissed as a neurological process.

When Patrick, who lives in Scotland, was seven he almost died during an emergency appendix operation. When he recovered he spoke of a place filled with golden light, music, perfume, flowers and beautiful birds. A lovely woman told him to go back as his mummy needed him. About a year later his mother was showing him an old photo album and he picked out his great-grandma as the woman 'who told me to go back the night I went to see God'.

Patrick had not seen a photo of the old woman before and his experience wasn't mentioned by anyone else at the time he picked her out. Children's Near Death Experiences usually involve a child seeing living rather than dead relatives. But in his case Patrick seemed to need a bit of loving grandmotherly advice to get him home safely for tea.

Gloria did know her father but her memory of him was very hazy. She told me:

'When I was six I became very ill with pneumonia and at one point almost died. It was then I saw my father, who had died when I was very young. Dad had been a policeman and now he was dressed in his uniform. I can still remember his shiny buttons as he carried me back from the beautiful place I had gone. My mother says I suddenly called out, "Oh Daddy," and that from that moment I started to get better.

'It wasn't surprising I saw my father, for though I had been so young we had been linked psychically. Indeed I had known the moment my father had died, though I was not more than two years old at the time. The family were getting ready to go and see my father, who was ill in hospital. Suddenly I cried and pointed, "Look, there's Daddy." Shortly afterwards the news came that my father had died just at the time I had called out.'

Deceased relatives are also seen when a person isn't actually dying but fears he may be. Such fears may be especially strong for a mother alone with her children.

Tricia was ill at home with very severe bronchitis. 'I couldn't breathe and went to the front gate just to get some fresh air. As I held on to the gate my dad, who had died over 20 years before, drove up in his old yellow car. Mum, who had died 10 years previously, was next to him. "Come on," Dad said, "get in the car. We've come to fetch you." "But I can't leave the children," I told him. "Don't worry then, we'll come another time," Dad replied.'

They were the words he might have used if Tricia had turned down a trip to the countryside. But from that moment she started to get better.

It is the very ordinary nature of these encounters that is for me their most significant factor – the odd heavenly choir and golden vision mixing with dad and mum popping by to see a sick daughter while out for a drive in their old yellow car. What is more, the appearance of a dead relative sometimes marks a turning point in an illness. Let scientists make what of it they will.

No one – not rationalists, scientists or theologians – can either prove or disprove the existence of life after death. But few of us deep down actually welcome the concept of simply ceasing to be. So it is reassuring that many people do have wonderful deathbed visions, often involving beloved relatives who have passed on before.

In the final days or even weeks, when perhaps a dying person is in pain, can we really offer anything better than the reassurance that life may end as it began, with those who love us waiting to greet us as they were at our birth? Not angels or demons but real people with real faults and real love? We don't know for sure what lies beyond this world, but death does not seem to part us from those we love. They come back with all the love, admonishment and advice they gave us in life.

I hope this book has made you laugh as well as cry so you'll see, from the stories I have told, that not only life but laughter goes on even in the very jaws of death. Nothing can take away the pain of losing a loved one. But no one can deny the everlasting power of love and family bonds.

My final story is like one of the first ones in this book, of Doris's mum who nagged her for not washing the greens. It is the tale of a mother who came back to take care of her son.

During the Second World War Monique was living with her family in Pondicherry, the former French enclave of India. 'My aunt Mimi, my father's sister, died in France just before the outbreak of the Second World War, and we had received no news at all about her two sons. Out of the blue one evening my youngest sister Denise, who was then a teenager, announced that she had seen our Aunty Mimi. Aunty Mimi had come to tell her that her son Roger was coming to stay with us.

'Two days later we received a telegram from Ceylon announcing that Roger would be arriving the next day.'

As I began I end by saying that it is the ordinary loving family concerns that in their way can tell us as much as any great philosophy. We may not always like our relatives – perhaps they know us too well – but woe betide anyone who criticizes them, for deep down we share with them an abiding and truly everlasting love.

Useful Addresses

I am always pleased to hear from readers and can be contacted through my publishers:

The Aquarian Press
HarperCollins*Publishers*
77–85 Fulham Palace Road,
Hammersmith, London W6 8JB.

The following addresses are of organizations I know to be supportive in times of sorrow.

BEREAVEMENT COUNSELLING
Bereavement Trust
Stanford Hall
Loughborough, Leics
LE12 5QR
Tel. 0509 852333

National network and umbrella advice for bereavement support services – a useful first contact.

Cruse – Bereavement Care
126 Sheen Road
Richmond-on-Thames
Surrey TW9 1UR
Tel. 081 940 4818

For one-to-one counselling and mutual support for all bereaved people. 200 branches nationwide. Telephone their central number for the branch nearest you, or send SAE for further details. They also have many excellent books for the bereaved of all ages.

Institute of Family Therapy
43 New Cavendish Street
London W1M 7RG
Tel. 071 935 1651

Free counselling to bereaved families or those with a very sick family member. (Donations welcomed.)

Jewish Bereavement Counselling Service
1 Cyprus Gardens
London N3 1SP
Tel. 081 349 0839 or 071 387 4300 ext. 227.

An opportunity to talk through one's grief with a trained Counsellor. Offers emotional support and help to members of the Jewish community.

Samaritans
A 24-hour-a-day phone line for all who despair. Look in the Yellow Pages for your local number.

You may wish to contact the minister, priest or leader of your local church or religious organization for help and support. Some ministers have special bereavement support groups within the parish, so it may be worth asking about.

BEREAVED PARENTS
The Compassionate Friends (support for bereaved parents)
6 Denmark Street
Clifton
Bristol BS1 5DQ
Tel. 0272 292778

Parents of Murdered Children Support Group
(a division of The Compassionate Friends)
46 Winters Way
Waltham Abbey
Essex EN9 3HP

Support through meetings, telephone calls and letters

SOS (Shadow of Suicide)
c/o The Compassionate Friends
6 Denmark Street
Clifton
Bristol BS1 5DQ
Tel. 0272 292778

INFANT DEATH COUNSELLING AND SHARED EXPERIENCE
Cot Death Helpline (24 hours a day)
071 235 1721

The Miscarriage Association
c/o Clayton Hospital
Northgate
Wakefield
West Yorks WF1 3JS
Tel. 0924 200799

For information and support

SANDS (Stillbirth and Neonatal Death Society)
28 Portland Place
London W1N 3DE
Tel. 071 436 5881

Many local groups

SAFTA (Support After Termination for Abnormality)
22 Upper Woburn Place
London WC1H 0CP
Tel. 071 387 7041

COUNSELLING AND OTHER THERAPIES
British Association for Counselling
1 Regent Place
Rugby
Warwicks CV21 2PJ
Tel. 0788 578328

Umbrella organization for counselling in Britain, with recognized code of ethics. The Counselling and Psychotherapy Resources Directory *(price £17) lists centres and practitioners nationwide. For free local information phone or write with an A5-sized SAE.*

Rebirthing
c/o Liz Cornish
Flat B
2 Wandsworth Common
London SW18 2EL
Tel. 081 870 9284

RELIGIOUS, SPIRITUAL AND PSYCHIC EXPERIENCES ASSOCIATIONS
You are assured of a warm welcome at any of the following organizations. Their membership is open to all and they can provide information, meeting places and a friendly ear.

Alister Hardy Research Centre for Religious and Spiritual Experience
Westminster College
Oxford OX2 9AT
Tel. 0865 243006

Churches Fellowship for Spiritual and Psychic Studies
44 High Street
New Romney
Kent TN28 8BZ
Tel. 0679 66937

The College of Psychic Studies
16 Queensberry Place
London SW7 2EB
Tel. 071 589 3292

The Scottish Society for Psychical Research
131 Stirling Drive
Bishopbriggs
Glasgow G64 3AX
Tel. 041 772 4588

SPIRITUAL HEALING
British Alliance of Healing Associations
Mrs Jo Wallace, Secretary
3 Sandy Lane
Gisleham
Lowestoft
Suffolk NR33 8EQ
Tel. 0502 742224

National Federation of Spiritual Healers
Old Manor Farm Studio
Church Street
Sunbury-on-Thames
Middlesex TW16 6RG
Tel. 0932 783164

SPIRITUALIST ORGANIZATIONS

It is very risky to get the name of a medium or clairvoyant out of your local paper. Contact an official association to ask for names of recognized, reliable mediums or for the addresses of spiritualist churches in your area – or for help or advice on any aspect of spiritualism.

Greater World Spiritualist Association
3–5 Conway Street
London W1P 5HP
Tel. 071 436 7555

130 affiliated churches

Spiritualist Association of Great Britain
33 Belgrave Square
London SW1 8QL
Tel. 071 235 3351

Spiritualist National Union
Redwoods
Stansted Hall
Stansted, Mounfitchet
Essex CM24 8UD
Tel. 0279 816363

400 spiritualist churches are affiliated with this organization.